Speaking
of
Journalism

BOOKS BY WILLIAM ZINSSER

Any Old Place with You
Seen Any Good Movies Lately?
The City Dwellers
Weekend Guests
The Haircurl Papers
Pop Goes America
The Paradise Bit
The Lunacy Boom
On Writing Well
Writing with a Word Processor
Willie and Dwike
Writing to Learn
Spring Training
American Places

BOOKS EDITED BY WILLIAM ZINSSER

Extraordinary Lives: The Art and Craft of American Biography
Inventing the Truth: The Art and Craft of Memoir
Spiritual Quests: The Art and Craft of Religious Writing
Paths of Resistance: The Art and Craft of the Political Novel
Worlds of Childhood: The Art and Craft of Writing for Children
They Went: The Art and Craft of Travel Writing

Speaking of Journalism

12 Writers and Editors Talk About Their Work

William Zinsser

and

Jennifer Allen, Melinda Beck,
Roger Cohn, Janice Kaplan,
Corby Kummer, Jane Mayer,
Kevin McKean, Lawrie Mifflin,
John S. Rosenberg, Mark Singer
and John Tierney

HarperPerennial
A Division of HarperCollinsPublishers

HarperCollins books may be purchased for educational, business, or sales promotional use. For information please write: Special Markets Department, HarperCollins Publishers, Inc., 10 East 53rd Street, New York, NY 10022.

First HarperPerennial edition published 1995.

Designed by Nancy Singer

The Library of Congress has catalogued the hardcover edition as follows:
Zinsser, William Knowlton.
    Speaking of journalism : 12 writers and editors talk about their work / by William Zinsser ; and Jennifer Allen . . . [et al.].
      p. cm.
   ISBN 0-06-270115-0
   1. Journalism. 2. Journalism—Vocational guidance. I. Title.
PN4775.Z48 1994
070—dc20   93-48753

ISBN 0-06-272064-3 (pbk.)
95 96 97 98 99 ❖/HC 10 9 8 7 6 5 4 3 2 1

CONTENTS

INTRODUCTION

During the 1970s I taught a course at Yale in nonfiction writing. My purpose was not to raise a new generation of journalists. I wanted to try to help students in every discipline to harness the world they were living in, and I selected my classes to be a mixture of young men and women from the various arts and sciences, bound for careers in various fields. I was looking for the next Rachel Carson or Lewis Thomas or David McCullough no less than the next White House correspondent.

But one of my students did turn out to be a White House correspondent, for *The Wall Street Journal*, and others went on to become successful writers and editors for newspapers and magazines ranging from *The New York Times* and the *New York Daily News* to *The New Yorker*, the *Atlantic*, *New York*, *Newsweek*, *Money*, *Rolling Stone*, *Audubon*, *Discover*, *Life*, *Vermont Magazine*, *Seventeen* and *Vogue*. Meanwhile I returned to New York and got back to my own writing. But I still did some teaching, and in the fall of 1992, when I decided to offer a nonfiction writing course at The New School, I hit on the idea of inviting some of my former Yale students to teach it with me. A different one would come each week and talk about his or her work. I made eleven phone calls, and nobody turned me down.

I wanted to teach at The New School because I've always liked its historic role: to provide information that helps motivated adults to get on with their lives. That's what I hoped my course would do, and I organized it to cover specific journalistic forms and skills that Yale students of mine excel at: feature writing, the personal column, scientific and technical writing, magazine editing, political and public affairs reporting, profiles, sportswriting, health and social-issues reporting, environmental and nature writing, and local and regional journalism. I taught the first session myself, to establish the principles that are important to me and that my students had taken into their own careers.

My instructions to them were simple. "Come and tell stories," I said. "Tell stories about what you do and how you do it, and how you got started, and what experiences you learned from, including your mistakes. Tell stories that illustrate a point about your kind of writing or editing—stories that aspiring writers will find helpful. If it's a good story, the class will remember the point. If the point isn't implicit, I'll be there, like Larry King, to drag you back to it or to make the point myself." Such prods were seldom necessary—as this book, which grew out of the class, proves. It's a book full of stories that are rich in useful detail. I saw my students turn into good teachers before my eyes.

I had also asked them to talk about values and not just about craft—such matters as fairness and accountability. I knew them all to be men and women of integrity, and the best questions asked by the class were ones that pursued ethical issues that the journalists raised, such as the growing tendency of reporters to color their stories with personal opinion or the tendency of magazine editors to rewrite and distort a writer's article to serve some agenda of their own.

This book is an act of reconstruction. I brought a tape recorder to class, and it provided my raw material, which was then transcribed. But conversational talk emerges on paper lacking much of the syntax and narrative coherence that the eye needs to process it and the mind needs to enjoy it, and I did extensive pruning and transposing and splicing and shaping. I also retained some classroom questions that led to an interesting answer. In several cases I went back to the teacher with my tape recorder and we made a fresh start, developing points I felt had been skimped or sidetracked or omitted. Throughout, my aim was to preserve the speaking voice of the person who taught the class. Then I sent the chapters to each of the teachers for their own revisions. The result isn't 100 percent true to what took place, but it's true to what we set out to teach and to what got taught. The class and the book are unidentical twins, each with its own personality.

Following each chapter I've written a postscript: an afterthought that occurred to me, often relating to some incident in my own career as a journalist. My purpose was to give the book a connecting thread, a reminder of its origins. But I also wanted to anchor it in an older journalistic tradition—older than the generation represented by eleven writers and editors just arriving at middle age. At Yale those men and women had been taught out of the values of my generation, and I in turn had been influenced by still earlier generations—as my postscripts, alluding to older mentors of mine at the *New York Herald Tribune* and to earlier models such as H. L. Mencken, gratefully acknowledge.

Like the rest of the book, my postscripts are personal and anecdotal. This is a book of voices. Listen, therefore, as you read. You will hear twelve journalists speaking of journalism—talking about how they work and what they believe.

New York
May, 1994

JOHN TIERNEY has been a general-assignment reporter for *The New York Times* since 1990, writing mainly for the Metro section. He also writes a column for *The New York Times Magazine*. Previously his career was with magazines—as a staff writer with *Science 80–84* and as a freelance writer reporting on science for *Discover*, *Esquire*, *Newsweek* and *Rolling Stone*. He wrote a humor column for *Health* magazine and contributed humor pieces to *Spy*, *Playboy*, the *Atlantic* and *Outside*. His work has appeared in three anthologies: *A Passion to Know*, *Newton at the Bat* and *Best Science Writing*. Among his awards are the *Washington Monthly* Journalism Award, for an article about the ill-fated attempt to build a nuclear-powered airplane, and the American Institute of Physics-United States Steel Foundation Science Writing Award, for an article about the equally ill-fated attempts to build a perpetual-motion machine. He lives in New York with his wife, Dana.

1

John Tierney

Feature Stories

For me the biggest challenge in feature writing is to find the angle—or, as it's sometimes called, the "take." Most stories originate with the idea that there is an interesting person or phenomenon or trend, and the trick is to think of a particular way to tell that story. A rule I try to remember—I've heard it attributed to the editor Byron Dobell—is that "a story should be a verb, not a noun." It shouldn't just be about a place or an institution; something should be happening there.

Early in my career as a magazine writer I got an assignment from *Esquire* that turned into a debacle. It was to write a story about Phil Knight, the founder of Nike. He was a man who had used a waffle iron in his garage to make the first sole of a running shoe that revolutionized the business. He was worth about $400 million. It seemed there ought to be something there to write about. But I never figured out what the take was; I never got beyond the nouns "Nike" or "Phil Knight." I couldn't even manage a simple profile, because when I went to see him I was unable to extract a single interesting quote. That's when I learned that the worst question an interviewer can ask is: "Can you tell me an interesting anecdote?" The person might have a million of them, but his mind will go absolutely blank. You can silence any raconteur with that question.

During that process my editor sent me a piece that Tom Wolfe had written for *Esquire* about Robert Noyce, who was one of the fathers of Silicon Valley. It began with the fact that Noyce grew up in Iowa and lived in Grinnell, a town that was founded by Protestants fleeing the sinful ways of the East; they went to Grinnell to start a new society. Wolfe's take was that these software engineers in modern California had the same attitude toward the East—they were puritans appalled by big New York corporations with extravagant hierarchies and lavish perquisites. In Silicon Valley it wasn't customary for the president of a company to have his reserved space in the parking lot. One day a visiting executive from New York was brought to the company by a chauffeur, who sat outside waiting, and the engineers were shocked that a company would assign one person to waste his time sitting in a car. It went against the religious values of Silicon Valley.

Anyway, that's how Wolfe saw it, and I remember resenting his story because it didn't have a quote from any software engineer saying that was how *he* saw Silicon Valley. It was all Tom Wolfe's idea. But later I came to think Wolfe was right to impose that perspective on the story. Even if the software engineers never talked about religion, Wolfe was justified in arriving at his own take on the subject, just as he had been entitled to say that astronauts had to have "the right stuff." I doubt if that phrase even occurred to the astronauts until they read Wolfe's book, and then they probably realized that he had captured the spirit of their program in a way they couldn't have.

In general, I think, the writer is more interesting than the person he or she is writing about. That sounds arrogant, and I don't mean that you shouldn't realistically portray the people you're covering or that you should intrude yourself into their story. But the reason you're a writer is that you have an interesting way of looking at situations. At least you have a fresh perspective. Most people who have been doing something for a long time become completely accustomed to the weirdnesses of their lives. You should always be faithful to representing how people feel, what they think and what they say. But I don't think you have to look at it from their point of view. That took me a long time to realize. I could hear the voices of the people I had interviewed saying, "That's not the way it is." And after a certain point I thought: I don't care; this is how *I* see it—which may be a more valid perspective.

I'll give you a small example. I did an article for my paper, *The New York Times*, about the boat basin at 79th Street on the Hudson River, which has been the subject of countless stories over the years describing the colorful bohemians and old salts who live there. My story compared them to the city's homeless squatters. These people were squatters on public land, which the city spent $2 million to fix up, and I wondered: Why do they have a right to stay there? The city is kicking the homeless out of the parks; why do these boat people have special rights? Well, my article got taped up on the fence at the boat basin and was annotated with 36 refutations. At one time that would have bothered me, but I knew that my facts were accurate and that my perspective was valid. The boat people had their own perspective: They had a right to be there because they had been there for ten years and it was only proper that the city should pay for them. But I think a more interesting question for the reader is: Why are your tax dollars going to give someone a low-rent place in a public park?

Q. Ten years ago, or even five years ago, would that approach have been allowed in a paper like the *Times*? You were hired as a reporter, but writers like you are increasingly being encouraged to write feature stories that embody an opinion, which is a groundswell change in American journalism.

I imagine it would have been more difficult to write that story ten years ago. True, I quoted the boat people's lawyer and their point of view, but I didn't give them 50 percent of the article. The gist of the piece was going toward "Why don't they pay any property taxes?"

Q. You mean you constructed the piece in such a way that the facts make your point? Your opinion, as such, never comes through?

Yes, and you can argue, I suppose, that that's disingenuous. But you're right about the trend. Newspapers are realizing that TV now provides much of the news—"Here's what happened today"—and that they have to come up with an approach to make themselves different. One example is the *Times*'s coverage this year [1992] of the presidential campaign, which was more daring than it had ever been before. Reporters were encouraged to look for fresh perspectives and to use distinctive voices. During the primaries I was assigned to sit in hotel rooms, watch television, and give my impression of what the campaign and the candidates looked like on the tube. My editors encouraged me to write with as much voice and opinion as I wanted. Eventually, after I wrote that Paul Tsongas came off as a "messianic pedant," they decided to label my stories "Campaign Watch," to alert readers that this was in the nature of a column, not a straight news story. But they told me to keep giving frank impressions. That kind of interpretive writing is much more important now to newspapers.

The most obvious way for a writer to approach any broad subject—any big institution or trend—is to find one person or place or event that stands for the whole story. Of course that's a cliché; there's even a word for it—it's called synecdoche. But in reporting many feature articles, the most important element is the considerable amount of time you spend trying to find the one person who makes a good story.

I was sent to Africa with another reporter to do a series about AIDS, the ultimate "noun" of a story. We had a whole continent and tons of statistics and studies, but we needed something specific—one tale. I went to Zambia, and I noticed that many articles about AIDS referred to a practice that was spreading the disease, called ritual cleansing. But the reference was always just one or two sentences. So I started asking about the practice. It wasn't an easy trail to follow; I would be in a village, and someone would know someone who had engaged in ritual cleansing, and they'd say, "You go about six miles and you'll see a big tree and then you turn left." Finally, in the capital city of Lusaka, someone put me onto a case. It took a week of badgering people before I got to that person's house, in a shantytown, but it turned into a good story. Here's how it starts:

LUSAKA, ZAMBIA—Sanford Mweupe now looks back wistfully on the uncomplicated days when he had only two wives to worry about. So do the two wives. Domestic life has been strained ever since the events delicately referred to in the household as "the confusion."

Last year, after his brother died, Mr. Mweupe was chosen by the family's elders to perform a ceremony called ritual cleansing. According to the tribal tradition, the brother's two widows had to be purged of their husband's spirit by having sex with a member of his family.

The problem was that Mr. Mweupe's brother had died of AIDS, and the widows quite possibly were infected as well. Mr. Mweupe's wives pleaded with him not to go ahead, but the elders insisted he cleanse the widows and then also take them as wives. He heard warnings from modern doctors, but a traditional healer assured him it would be safe.

So Mr. Mweupe became confused—a not uncommon reaction on a continent where a virus has suddenly intruded into tens of millions of lives. Fatal diseases are never simple anywhere, but it is hard to imagine any quite as complex as AIDS in Africa.

In places like this capital city, where it appears that a fifth of adults are infected, AIDS is a family disease that touches virtually everyone in some way. It confronts Africans not only with death but with challenges to their cultural foundations: their ancestral beliefs, their marital roles and familial obligations, their conceptions of morality and sexuality.

"What could I do?" Mr. Mweupe, a soft-spoken 52-year-old, said one recent afternoon in his living room. "I was bound by tradition."

Once I found that man, it was fairly straightforward to tell his story and give readers a vivid look at what was happening in Africa. All the effort was in finding him.

At one point I was assigned to do some pieces about the Times Square redevelopment—another noun, and a vague one. I came upon a building, at the corner of 42nd Street and Broadway, where the tenants were being evicted. It was almost empty, and I just went in and wandered around, and there, separately, I came upon two ancient Times Square institutions—the radio host Joe Franklin and a press agent named Dick Falk. On one level those were easy stories, once I found the two men—the idea of these two entrenched Broadway types getting kicked out. The problem was to find a fresh way of looking at them. God really is in the details in this kind of story.

Joe Franklin has been written about forever. But to me the funny thing—my take on it—was that the city is trying to clean up Times Square, and it has to get Joe Franklin, who has the messiest office in the world, to move. I don't claim that this take was a revolutionary insight—you might think it was so obvious as to be trite. But at least it gave me a way to write about Joe Franklin and the redevelopment of Times Square. It enabled me to select which details to mention and which quotes to use. When you have a lot of quotes from people who talk at great length, you have to choose the right ones. In Joe's office everything in the world was there, and trying to convey that was what I loved:

The New York State Urban Development Corporation has achieved a major triumph in its long and troubled campaign to clean up Times Square. This week its lawyers are forcing Joe Franklin to clean out his office.

Mr. Franklin is renowned as Broadway's greatest nostalgist and television's most durable host—his 39-year-old syndicated talk show is listed in the *Guinness Book of World Records*—but some acquaintances think his most remarkable achievement is the clutter in his one-room office. The debris sits above the northeast corner of Broadway and 42nd Street, in a building whose tenants are being evicted to make room for a new office tower.

The mounds of coffee cups and unanswered letters long ago engulfed the desk and surrounding floor, squeezing Mr. Franklin and his secretary into a clearing by the doorway with one chair. They would take turns sitting. They kept working there this week as movers began carting off, among other things, 12,500 sheets of vaudeville music, 10,000 movie reels, and an undetermined number of unopened press releases from the Eisenhower era.

"I've told them not to throw out anything," said Franklin, who is 62 years old. "The key word to me is 'someday.' It's my solace: someday I'll get to it. This way I also get a thrill that a neat man can never have—the thrill of finding something that was irretrievably lost."

He rummaged through a pile and found a shopping bag where he had filed a 1971 issue of *The New Yorker*, which had a profile of him, called "Broadway Joe." He pointed to the description of his office: "It has that quality that goes beyond mere grime and disorder." Mr. Franklin nodded happily. "I love that description," he said.

Mr. Franklin said he thought of the room as the "prototype of what an office should not be," and his secretary, Sophia Orkoulas, agreed. Ms. Orkoulas, a 21-year-old actress, looked surprised when asked to describe her filing system.

"Well, we don't have drawers where you keep paper inside and stuff like that," she explained. "There really isn't much of a system. We just remember what section of the floor we put something. I thought about organizing things once, but this is the way Joe likes it."

Ms. Orkoulas said there wasn't really any need for a supply cabinet because there were not really any supplies. When they needed a pen or a paper clip they rummaged on the floor for a used one, and when they needed to write something they could always find an old letter or an announcement with an unused side.

"We used to have some blank sheets of paper," she said, "but we ran out."

The secretary said all that with an absolutely straight face. It's only when you go back and look at your notes that you realize how absurd it is.

Q. But what makes the piece work is all the statistical detail— the 12,500 pieces of sheet music; it's not "some," or "a lot of," or "a couple of hundred." The numbers are tremendously vivid. So is the detail that they take turns sitting on the one chair. You need an eye for humorous detail to notice that and to use it. Do you remember how it happened to come up?

I was looking for a place to sit, and Joe Franklin said, "You can use the chair." His secretary just stood up and gave it to me. To them it was perfectly natural that an office would have only one chair, and by then it almost seemed natural to me too—it's easy to get so acclimated to an environment that you stop noticing its peculiarities. But later, as I was writing the story, away from that den of chaos, I realized that it was a funny detail.

I had a similarly chaotic experience with the other tenant in the building, Dick Falk, whom I later wrote about in another story. He was a man who could talk happily for three hours straight—one disjointed story after another. I walked out of his office exhausted; I didn't know how I was going to produce anything coherent from the interview. But later something occurred to me as I was telling friends about Falk. By the way, that's often a good way to figure out the take. As you tell your friends about a story, notice which details interest them and which direction you find yourself following. Anyway, in talking about Falk I found myself focusing on how amazed and delighted he was to have a reporter wander uninvited into his office. For once this PR man wasn't out there begging for publicity, but he was making news anyway because he was the last tenant in the building. And it occurred to me, as I waded through all the ridiculous press releases he had given me, that it was odd he hadn't written a press release about this reasonably newsworthy situation. So that theme became the frame of my story. It began with a straightforward two-paragraph lead, followed by the longest sentence I've ever gotten into the *Times:*

The 12 floors of the Longacre Building are empty these days except for the security guards and Richard R. Falk. He is the same age as the building, 79, and has been known for decades as the mayor of 42nd Street. He opposes the $2.5-billion revelopment of Times Square, which is supposed to begin with the demolition of his building, and he has refused to move out of his one-room office on the third floor.

What Mr. Falk has done so far during his solitary entrenchment against the New York State Urban Development Corporation's project makes for a moderately unusual story. But what he has not done so far is truly extraordinary.

So far Mr. Falk, who proudly claims to be the model for the loathsome public-relations man in *Sweet Smell of Success,* who currently estimates that he has generated five tons of press clippings and supplied gossip columnists with made-up quotes from 10,000 clients, who in his quest for publicity has carried a cross up Broadway, dressed a model in a bikini of frankfurters, gotten March 21 declared "Fragrance Day" and tried to check a trained flea named The Great Herman into the Waldorf-Astoria Hotel—so far Mr. Falk, by his own admission, has not sent out a single press release about his plight....

"It's just facts," he said disdainfully of his situation. "It's 100 percent real. I can't write a press release for that. You need a press agent when you have something that's 50 percent real. You make it a little fantastic or humorous, bring in enough pseudo-facts, and the papers will buy it. I always say that everything I write is guaranteed to be 50 percent true."

The article goes on to recall some of Falk's publicity exploits, brought off with his self-described "demonic frenzy" on behalf of legions of Broadway restaurants, nightclubs and would-be celebrities, and concludes by going back to the opening theme:

"The press is coming to me," he said. "I just can't believe it. All my life I'm looking for space in the papers, I'm dying for it, and now it's falling on me. Without creating anything, I'm in *The New York Times!* To be in the *Times*—you're immortal, almost. Do you know how many millionaires would die to get a story in the *Times*? It took me 50 years, but I made it. I'm going out in style. This is it. This is my epitaph."

He was asked if he had any suggestions for how the epitaph should read. Of course he did.

"Famed Flack Who Exploited and Promoted Stars and Shows Finally Gets His Reward."

In writing feature articles it's important to be able to change directions. The best stories are often the ones that surprise you. Writers tend to go into stories with a preconceived idea and to stick with it. I try to remind myself to stay flexible. When the world chess championship between Karpov and Kasparov was held at the Macklowe Hotel, an editor at the *Times* got the idea: Just go over there and see what it's really like, these two guys locked in combat. Just go watch them. I went, and all I saw was two guys sitting at a table. I couldn't come up with anything to say. Later I was hanging around the hotel's pressroom, where the grandmasters gather, and it struck me that what was much more interesting was the kibitzing going on—all these guys sitting next door and commenting on the the moves. So I stole an idea from one of my favorite books, *One-upmanship*, by Stephen Potter, and wrote a piece about chess kibitzing—tips on how to kibitz, which I gleaned from some of the grandmasters in the room:

"Always give yourself an escape," said Bruce Pandolfini. "If you're not sure whether a move is good or not, say, 'That's interesting' or 'That's worth taking a look at.' If it really looks wrong, say, 'I'm not *quite* sure that's sound.' You can get away with saying that a move gives a 'spatial edge' or a 'powerful attacking position' as long as you don't specify what edge or what attack. Or you can just generalize with something like 'Black seems rather defensive here.' How can anyone argue with that? It may not mean anything."

One of the men in the room was pretty funny. He was a grandmaster from Detroit, named Eric Schiller. His advice was to recall chess games from the past, but selectively:

"When everyone else is puzzling over a situation that's arisen," he said, "you suddenly announce, 'Oh, I remember this position. It was played three weeks ago in Kuala Lumpur by Belyavsky and Portisch.' It's good to use one Russian name and one European name and to stick to an out-of-the-way place. Reykjavik is another good choice." If by some remote chance another kibitzer begs to differ, Mr. Schiller suggests a casual, "Well, perhaps it was a slightly different position, but it had the same idea."

Q. Many people are funny, but you have an ear for hearing it when it comes along. There has always been a current of humor running through your work, but it's not just for the sake of being funny. You've been reading us some very funny things that people have said, and yet they are beyond funny—they are pertinent to the story. Are you very patient as a reporter?

In the case of humor, you often have to wait them out and drag it out of them. You have to just keep asking questions over and over in many different ways. What I give myself credit for in that chess story is the idea of asking those kibitzers, "What are the rules of kibitzing?" As soon as they heard it they got excited. I also called a lot of other people—heads of chess clubs in different parts of the country—and asked them. Many of them couldn't think of any rules, but a few got into the spirit as I egged them on.

Q. To go back to your original point: What makes that an entertaining piece is your idea. It's not the story you were sent out to cover.

Right, and I was lucky enough to have an editor who was open to a different story. That's not always the case. There are editors who not only insist that they know exactly what the story is; they also think they know exactly how to write it. A friend of mine got an assignment from a magazine editor who told him that the story had to begin with three anecdotes, then state the theme, then have a section about this and a section about that. Such formulas are stifling to the writer—and ultimately, of course, to the reader. If you can plot the story so explicitly before you do any reporting, how interesting or surprising can it be?

But good editors realize that the best stories are the ones they didn't ask for. They realize that *they're* not out there on the street. When I sit in on story idea meetings at the *Times*, it's interesting to see the situation from the editor's perspective. Someone might make an offhand suggestion that will turn into a story idea after 20 seconds of discussion. Obviously the editors don't know much about the topic or how the story's going to turn out; they only know that it's an interesting topic, and they trust the reporter to find the right angle. They realize that the reporter knows more than they do, and they can be dissuaded if you come back and say, "There's no story there." But of course it's always better if you can then suggest another story—one that you *did* find.

Often all you have to do is look at something from a slightly different perspective. I was assigned to write about a self-defense course in which women learn to fight off attacks from someone called a "model mugger"—a guy in a helmet and a padded suit who pretends to be a rapist and gets kicked and punched as he attacks the women. Many stories have been written in newspapers and magazines about these classes, and they always stress how empowering the course is for the women students. It occurred to me that nobody has taken the perspective of the model mugger. What's it like to have a job in which you go to work and get beaten up all day long? So that was my take. Another possibility, if I had wanted to write in the first person, would have been to put on the mugger's outfit and get beaten up myself. I didn't do it because I felt that the mugger's experienced perspective would be more interesting than my first impressions.

But sometimes you have to be more active in shaping the story, and maybe even get involved in it yourself. That happened with my piece about Monty Hall, host of the TV game show *Let's Make a Deal*, and what has come to be known as the "three-door problem." The *Times* ran the story on page 1, which is an indication of how intriguing the problem is; mathematicians have called it the "Monty Hall problem" since it was analyzed in *American Statistician* in 1976. A few years ago *Parade* magazine ran an article about the problem, which started a huge controversy and drew hundreds of letters. The problem has also been tested in more than a thousand schools, at every level from second grade to graduate school, and people still argue about it. That's what interested me.

The problem, as you may know, is that the contestant is shown three doors. One door has a car behind it; the other two have goats. The contestant picks, say, No. 1, and Monty Hall, who knows what's behind the other doors, opens No. 3, which has a goat. He then asks if the contestant wants to pick No. 2 instead. The question is: Is it to the contestant's advantage to switch? Everyone's intuitive feeling is that the odds are 50 percent either way. Which, it turns out, they're not; there's an advantage if you switch. But I had to think of a way to why that was so, and it took me the longest time.

Finally it came to me: Why not go to Monty Hall's house and play the game with *him*? He lives in Beverly Hills, and the *Times* was sending me to Mexico to write about some eclipse watchers, so that's when the solution began to fall into place. Because, as I realized when I got to talking with Hall, it isn't solely a problem of mathematical probability. It has another element, which is the motivation of the host. So only Monty Hall could answer that question.

Using me as the contestant, Hall set up the game on his dining room table and we ran 20 trials based on the theories of all those people who had written letters to *Parade*. At that point the problem began to catch Hall's imagination, and he suggested a new set of trials:

On the first, the contestant picked Door No. 1. "That's too bad," Mr. Hall said, opening Door No. 1. "You've won a goat."

"But you didn't open another door or give me a chance to switch."

"Where does it say I have to let you switch every time? I'm the master of the show. Here, try it again."

On the second trial the contestant again picked Door No. 1. Mr. Hall opened Door No. 3, revealing a goat. The contestant was about to switch to Door No. 2 when Mr. Hall pulled out a roll of bills. "You're sure you want Door No. 2?" he asked. "Before I show you what's behind the door I will give you $3,000 in cash not to switch to it."

"I'll switch to it."

"Three thousand dollars," Mr. Hall repeated, shifting into his famous cadence. "Cash. Cash money. It could be a car, but it could be a goat. Four thousand."

"I'll try the door."

"Forty-five hundred. Forty-seven hundred. Forty-eight. My last offer: Five thousand dollars."

"Let's open the door."

"You just ended up with a goat," he said, opening the door.

Mr. Hall continued: "Now do you see what happened there? The higher I got, the more you thought the car was behind Door No. 2. I wanted to con you into switching there, because I knew the car was behind 1. That's the kind of thing I can do when I'm in control of the game. You may think you have probability going for you, but there's the psychological factor to consider."

He proceeded to prove his case by winning the next eight rounds....

Was Mr. Hall cheating? Not according to the rules of the show, because he did have the option of not offering the switch, and he usually didn't offer it...."If the host has the choice whether to allow a switch or not, beware," Hall concluded. "Caveat emptor. It all depends on his mood."

The *Times* ran the story along with an explanatory box, called "To Switch or Not to Switch," and I got hundreds of letters—the biggest reaction I've ever gotten to a story—from people who said, "You moron, you don't understand the problem." Finally I was reduced to saying, "All right, come to New York and bring some money and we'll play the game." Unfortunately, nobody took me up.

POSTSCRIPT

WILLIAM ZINSSER • It's not necessary to be Irish to write good feature stories, but maybe it helps. Listening to John Tierney, I was reminded of a *New York Herald Tribune* reporter named John O'Reilly, who was much admired for his deadpan coverage of human-interest and animal-interest subjects, and that in turn reminded me of how I got started as a journalist myself. As a boy, I never wanted to grow up to be a writer, or—God forbid—an author. I wanted to be a newspaperman, and the newspaper I wanted to be a man on was the *Herald Tribune*. Reading it every morning, I loved the tremendous sense of enjoyment it conveyed. All the people who put out that paper, with its beautiful Bodoni Bold layouts—editors, writers, photographers, makeup men—were having a wonderful time; I felt that they were putting out the paper just for me. Articles in the *Trib* almost always had some extra touch of grace or humanity or humor—some gift of themselves that the writers enjoyed making to their readers. To be one of those editors and writers, I thought, would be the American boy's ultimate dream.

That dream came true in 1946, when I got home from the war and talked my way onto the *Herald Tribune* staff. My salary was $40 a week, and I felt as rich as Rockefeller—or, at least, I was having more fun. I brought with me my belief that a sense of enjoyment is a crucial ingredient in writing and editing, and I was now in the same room with the journalists who first put that idea in my head. The great reporters like Homer Bigart wrote with warmth and gusto, and the great critics and columnists like Virgil Thomson and Red Smith wrote with elegance and with a mirthful confidence in their irreverent opinions. On the "split page"—as the first page of the second section was called, when papers had only two sections—the political column by Walter Lippmann, America's most venerated pundit, ran above the one-panel cartoon by H. T. Webster, creator of "The Timid Soul," who was also an American institution. I liked the insouciance that presented on the same page two features so different in gravity. Nobody thought of hustling Webster off to the "comics" section. Both men were giants, part of the same equation.

Among those blithe souls, John O'Reilly, a city desk reporter, managed to make whimsy a serious beat. I fondly remember his annual story about the woolly bear—the caterpillar whose brown and black stripes are said to foretell by their width whether the coming winter will be harsh or mild. Every fall O'Reilly would go to Bear Mountain Park, along with the photographer Nat Fein, best known for his Pulitzer Prize-winning shot of Babe Ruth's farewell at Yankee Stadium, to observe a sample of woolly bears crossing the road, and his article was written in mock-scientific museum-expedition style, duly portentous. The paper always ran the story at the bottom of page 1, under a three-column head, along with a one-column cut of a woolly bear, its stripes none too distinct. In the spring O'Reilly would write a follow-up piece explaining whether the woolly bears had been right, and nobody blamed him or them if they had been wrong. The main thing was to give everyone a good time.

When I was teaching at Yale I invited the humorist S. J. Perelman, near the end of his life, to come up and talk to my students, and one of them asked him, "What does it take to be a comic writer?" He said, "It takes audacity, and exuberance, and gaiety, and the most important one is audacity." Then he said, "The reader has to believe that the writer is feeling good."

JENNIFER ALLEN started writing for magazines when she was seventeen—for *Seventeen*. She has been a reporter for *Life* and the *New York Daily News* and has written freelance columns and pieces for *The New York Times*, *New York*, *Esquire*, *GQ*, *Mademoiselle*, *McCall's* and other magazines. She lives in New York with her husband and nine-year-old daughter and is forever at work on a piece of fiction.

2

THE PERSONAL COLUMN

About a year after I graduated from college I got a job as a reporter at *Life*, which was then being reborn as a monthly. I loved reporting, and after a while I was lucky enough to get a chance to write my own text blocks—the extended captions that accompany the photographs. The Time Inc. magazines were top-heavy with editors, and the editing process was laborious. The text blocks would go through a copy editor, one or two senior editors, an assistant managing editor, the managing editor, and then upstairs to Henry Grunwald, Time Inc.'s editor in chief, and each of them would want something different done. The writer would get six versions back and make all the changes and send the piece on its way one last time. I remember an editor coming into the copy-room late one night when a piece was closing. "Is it dead yet?" he asked. By then the text blocks had often lost the bite or individuality or humor that the writer put into them.

I had a lot of youthful energy, and I was restless. I wanted to write, and under this collective editing process one article could be in the works for months, from conception to closing. Another editor, Byron Dobell, who had come to *Life* from *Esquire* and other writer-oriented magazines, was also impatient with the group-journalism method of doing things; in fact, he never did make peace with it, and pretty soon he left. Byron encouraged me to do some writing on my own.

So one day I sat down and tried to write about my childhood. I had never done that before, and I didn't know what was going to come out. But Byron was very spirited and impractical, in a wonderful way, and he said, "Just write what you want to write and *then* worry about whether you can get it published." That was tremendously liberating—to just write something in my own voice. It turned out to be a voice I had never used before. It was a credulous memory voice—not a voice that imitated a child's voice, but one that remembered the sensation of what it was like to be a child. It seemed heartfelt, and it caught me by surprise.

Until then I had always taken a journalistic stance, in which the writer gives the appearance of knowing everything. Which, actually, happened to connect with a strong strain in my personality. At *Life* I was a fanatical researcher; once, when I compiled notes for a piece about Donny Osmond, I wrote the equivalent of a book about the Osmond family. But this personal column was about confusion and sadness and about not "getting it" as a child—just the opposite of a piece by a powerful journalist. It was about me being a small, powerless person, full of wonder and awe at the grownups, and when it later ran as a "Hers" column in *The New York Times* it got a huge response. I saw that this voice I still had inside me and had been afraid to use—a voice that was innocent and credulous and open to disappointment—could be an effective one.

The column was about my parents' cocktail parties. It was material I barely remembered, from when I was about seven—like walking around those parties in my pajamas, or wearing the slippers my father had brought home from an Indian reservation—and I put all those dim memories of all those parties into a column about one cocktail party. I wrote,

for instance, that my brother and sister didn't like those parties and were in the basement watching Don Ameche on television. Whether they were actually watching Don Ameche
didn't matter to me, and that was also very liberating, because
at *Life* we had to put a red dot over every word to confirm
that it was factually correct. In writing this piece I came to
understand that I wasn't going to get in trouble if Don
Ameche wasn't on TV that particular night; the piece was
true in a larger sense.

That's something any fiction writer knows. But I was a
timid, straight-arrow girl; everything I had gotten out of life
was a reward for being correct, for red-dotting. The idea that
I might evoke a cocktail party without being strictly factual
was subversive—the idea that everything would be in the
details but that it didn't matter if it was on this night or some
other night that my father's friend got drunk and threw a
punch bowl across the room. Something more important was
being addressed, which was how the party *felt*.

The column begins with my father moving out of the
house and leaving us. I remembered that my parents had a lot
of drinking equipment, so I just began by listing all those
objects. Gradually I realized that the piece didn't have to be
about the equipment—that I could use the list as a diving
board and dive off and do something else. When that happened I thought: Now it's going to be hard to go back to red-
dotting. Here are a few paragraphs:

What I remember best about my father's departure is
what he left behind. And what he left behind, apart from
two volumes of Peter Arno cartoons and several John Gun-
ther books, were party supplies, the stuff that defined my
parents as active members of the young marrieds' suburban
cocktail party scene, circa 1960–65, a scene that vanished
from our house the day he left.

From time to time while I was growing up I used to
take out the artifacts from their resting places in cupboards
and drawers and study them, those icons of a previous
slaphappy civilization: cut-crystal glasses; for old-fash-

ioneds; tall, frosted gin-and-tonic glasses; and skinny, slim-stemmed martini glasses—a whole cupboardful of glasses for holding liquor.

Left behind, too, was all the cocktail party music, the albums they'd played at their parties: Ray Conniff and Dave Brubeck and *Ella Fitzgerald Sings Cole Porter* and Frank Sinatra's *Songs for Young Lovers....*

Our living room is crammed with the flush-faced 30-year-old men in sports jackets and shined-up penny loafers. With them are their wives, in scoop-necked cocktail dresses and big stiff hairdos. Through the vapory clouds of cigarette smoke I can make out my mother, the most glamorous woman in the world, a hundred times prettier than Elizabeth Taylor or Peggy Lee....

What the column finally turned out to be about was the end of the suburban culture of my parents and their friends. That culture was my childhood—or at least what I perceived as my childhood and what I remembered of the grownups—so the column was also about the end of my childhood. It was also about loss. It was also about families, and of course it was also about my parents. I remember being pleased when I wrote that my mother was prettier than Peggy Lee, because that's exactly what I thought at the time—she was so beautiful, and who could be more beautiful than Peggy Lee? Again, it wasn't the writing voice of an all-knowing adult; it was the credulous voice that we're supposed to outgrow but that we probably never entirely lose.

That first column touched universal truths—which is fundamental to writing a successful personal column or essay. Just the other day a book came in the mail from a woman who said, "I read that piece of yours many years ago and it inspired me to write this novel." Most of the letters I got were from women my age who had had a similar experience, not necessarily of a divorce in the family but of some half-forgotten childhood memory. I think they liked the description of the era, though it wasn't a sweetly nostalgic column; on the contrary, it was quite rueful.

But more than that, I think they liked the voice, that all-believing voice: being a child and thinking your parents were wonderful and their parties were wonderful and the hi-fi was so glamorous because it had those little gold threads in the webbing, and it probably was *real gold*, and then one day it ends, and you're not ready for it—nobody told you it was going to be over between 11 and 12 in the morning. Which, in one way or another, happens to everybody. Your parents are the best parents in the world, and then suddenly they're not, and they can never go back to being those parents, and you can never get that time back.

Another column from that same period got a big response, for many of the same reasons. My editors at the *Times* said, "Nobody has been able to write about sex for the 'Hers' column," and they wanted me to try. Thinking about it, I certainly wasn't going to write an out-and-out piece on sex, which would have been mortifying. The only thing I could think of was to recall hearing about sex when I was young—in this case, ten or eleven. To be a child in the '60s was to be in a culture that was suddenly saturated with sex; it was in the air. The point of my column was that although I was hazy about the details, sex was this thing that permeated everything. If you stayed up late you could hear Johnny Carson making jokes about it, and Hugh Hefner was everywhere—everybody knew what *Playboy* bunnies were but not exactly what they did—and Marilyn Monroe was everywhere. My mother was so sad when Marilyn Monroe died, and that memory was also a part of what I wrote about. I was too young to quite get it. I thought: she died because she was too sexy.

So sex was this incredibly potent force, and at the same time there was a disparity between that fact—that sex was somehow dangerous or menacing or thrilling or exciting or exotic—and what you learned in gym class, which was that it was dry and clinical and scientific. The truth, as I eventually resolved it, was that sex was probably closer to this other hinted-at thing: that it was filled with innuendo and mystery.

As a child you thought that if you shook hands with a boy you were going to have a baby, because it was in the air. On some level that metaphor is true—it *is* in the air; you *can* catch it. You can't have a baby by letting a boy pull your ponytail, but they're connected.

I loved writing that column because, again, the voice was true to who I had been at a certain age, and judging by the response, it was true to all young girls in the '60s. It made a connection. Not long after that I began to write columns out of my actual age, about what I was thinking in my early twenties. But I had been liberated by those previous columns—by the knowledge that what I had to say about my own life and my own emotions was valid not only for myself but for other people.

If it works, it's all about the voice, and you can't fake that. You can look to other writers for inspiration, but you can't become those writers. I still remember Joan Didion's column about Hawaii, but it really wasn't about Hawaii; it was about *her* in Hawaii. Finally it almost doesn't matter what you're writing about. People don't read your column to find out about something in the world; you're not required to wrap it all up and proclaim some great truth. They're reading you because they want to spend some time with you as a friend, to find out what you think. It's like having a cup of coffee with someone you like.

But however simple these columns may seem, you don't get away with anything. I found that out. Sometimes an editor will call from a magazine that nobody you know is going to see, and you say to yourself—not cynically but just pragmatically—"Twelve hundred bucks? I need a new rug. O.K., I'll do it." Invariably, when I did that, if I ever tried to just knock off a column, I'd get a call from the editor saying, "Something's missing in this piece." I'd get very upset, and I'd think: Who is this editor in Tennessee? How does *she* know something's missing? And then I'd read the piece again, and it was true. There was a hole. What's missing is that you can't write a personal column without going to some very deep place inside yourself, even if it's only for four hours. It's almost like psychotherapy, except that you're doing it on your own. You have to pull something out of yourself and give away some important part of yourself. If you don't . . . well, I was never able to sell a piece that didn't put me through that process. I always had to (as the editors would say) run it through the typewriter again.

Sometimes I'd think: This is hardly worth it—it's just a column about how much your feet hurt when you're pregnant. But if you're not connecting to something that was painful, or that's hard for you to admit, or that maybe you're ashamed of or embarrassed about, it's not going to work. It's a gift you have to give the reader, even if it's the most light-hearted piece in the world. You can't be dishonest, much as I'd like to be. I hate it when editors make me cut out my passages from Flaubert. They say, "Those passages from Flaubert really don't fit in with the rest of the piece," and I think: but that's the good part; that's the part that shows how smart I am. You don't get away with it.

If your column has an agenda—if it's anything other than an honest appraisal of what you think—the reader is going to smell it. If your agenda is to be vindictive, or to make fun of somebody, why would a reader want to spend time with someone who is cruel? That's also true of a column that's high-handed, or a column that preaches. Just as in life you can't tell somebody how to change, or how to act, or that they should give up smoking—they'll do it when they're ready to do it—you can't tell the reader how to be. In fact, I found that if you go around telling people "Do this" and "Do that," the problem isn't with them; it's with you.

I wrote a column for *Child* magazine about child-rearing experts. This was after I had a child of my own. It was going to be such a funny piece: about how those experts don't know anything. It was me being smart-alecky. My approach to the reader was: "I'm too smart for all this doubt and uncertainty that all these other mothers need help with in raising their children, and so are you, so let's take a stroll through some of these advice books and make fun of them." Well, I wrote the piece, and the editor called back and sounded very cool. I thought about it, and it dawned on me that I had actually learned a lot from child-rearing experts, especially Leonard Balkin, who had a three-hour radio show every Saturday morning that I never missed. All the parents who called in to that show had the same questions I had; I felt I was part of this community and needed it. Yet here I was trying to write about how stupid all this advice was.

Partly, I guess, it was a kind of snobbery. But mainly I think it was because I was embarrassed about my own neediness. There was plenty to make fun of in those books and on that radio show; some of those parents said amazing things. But something else was happening on the show that went beyond all that—something that was true—and my piece was flat because I tried to separate myself from all those other parents. In fact I wasn't that different from them. I had a great deal in common with their uncertainty and their anxiety and with all people who are trying to raise a child. I got my article back from the magazine and turned it completely around.

Writing a personal column for the wrong reason is a big hazard. I used to get calls five or six times a year from editors asking me to do a piece on what it's like to be married to an older person, as I am. When you're a freelancer, if you're young and ambitious, you get rather feverish, so I'd sit at the typewriter and think: Could I possibly make a go of this? You never want to say no to an editor. But that was when I began to learn to say no. Even *I* could never bring myself to write that column. Editors seldom seem to realize that it's going to be your name on the piece—that you're going to be mortified about it, that it's too intimate. But as a writer it's often hard to make that judgment; writing is what you do, and the lines get blurry. You lose discretion.

Several times when I was younger I allowed editors to tamper with my work and my integrity. Once, for a feature article in a newspaper, I was assigned to write about a woman whose publicist, it turned out, had done something to annoy my editor, and after I wrote the interview he made me go back and make it meaner—really mean. Which, I'm sorry to say, I did. Then, inconveniently enough, I ran into that woman. It was the writer's nightmare. She came over and said, "Why did you do that to me?" I said, "I'm sorry. You're right. An unfortunate thing happened at the office, and I felt I had no choice." She said the piece had really hurt her feelings, and I thought: I got off easy; if she had come over and socked me on the jaw that would have been all right, because she really wasn't a horrible person. I not only violated her; I violated myself.

Subsequently I spent a year writing personal columns for *New York* magazine, and I had one editor who was much more arch than I was. I wrote a piece about an ex-Weatherman named Bill Ayres, who was running a day-care center on the Upper West Side. It was a wonderful day-care center, and I became fond of him and admired his values. He was a dedicated teacher, and my story, which was quite affectionate, had a sort of sadness for the passing of the '60s. Part of him was still living in that decade; he was doing his best, working with small children all day long for almost no money. Well, my editor ran the piece through *her* typewriter, and it came out very snide and mean-spirited. It made brutal fun of Bill Ayres, and of the children at his day-care center, and of any parents who would send their child there. But I let it go. I was new to the magazine, and I thought maybe it was a rule that you wrote your column and somebody else rewrote it. I've regretted it ever since, and I never let it happen again.

Today I'd say that if you find yourself writing for a magazine that doesn't value your voice or your point of view, look for one that does. There are plenty around. It doesn't matter what the magazine is, or what it's about. If it has an editor who is listening to you and is fair with you and is paying you, you should cherish that more than all the exposure in the world. What matters is your work. It's *your* work. Finally you don't have to do any kind of writing that you don't want to do.

But that's probably the hardest lesson of all to learn.

WILLIAM ZINSSER • "You lose discretion" is the sentence that lingers with me from Jennifer Allen's class. How often I've had young or aspiring writers tell me they let themselves be pushed by an editor in a direction that violated their integrity, or allowed their piece to be rewritten to satisfy a magazine's notion of what the story should say and how it should be slanted. Squeezed between compromising their standards and not being published, the writers felt that they had to comply, and it's hard to blame them. Two powerful drives are at work on all of us who write. One is the urge to see our words in print. The other is the need to pay the bills. Writers, like artists and musicians, sacrifice solvency for their art. They live at risk, vulnerable to editors who have an agenda of their own. You lose discretion.

The editor who told Jennifer Allen to make her article meaner has a name that is well known in journalism—I've withheld it to protect the guilty. He has long edited a succession of aggressive magazines, and I can only wonder how much damage he and other such editors have caused, not only to young writers but to the people those writers have thereby victimized, like the day-care-center operator whose life-affirming story, as initially written by Jennifer Allen, turned to ashes when it was rewritten by a *New York* editor who was "more arch" than she was.

Two years ago a general-assignment reporter named Donald E. Skinner, leaving newspaper work after 20 years with papers in Kansas and California, wrote a farewell letter to his colleagues at *The Orange County Register* (California), explaining why he had quit. His letter was widely circulated, and one of the places it landed, where I saw it, was in the *Columbia Journalism Review*:

. . . I have spent years coaxing people into saying negative things about other people. I have harassed officers of the law and politicians who were only doing their jobs. I have persistently coaxed quotes and color photos out of bereaved family members and dwelled lovingly on animal stories while ignoring the plight of the homeless. I have overwritten stories with the encouragement of editors, underwritten stories with the encouragement of editors, stirred up controversies where none should have existed, used words to divide neighborhoods and families, and rushed stories into print without all the facts in order to meet an artificial deadline.

I have begged sources for long interviews, then used two sentences that trivialized their research. I have joked about human tragedy, spent hours on the phone with jail inmates and gun nuts, asked inane questions of erudite sources to satisfy an editor's childlike curiosity, and delved into the private lives of drunks, murderers, child molesters, politicians and priests. I have hung around outside funeral homes. I have exaggerated weather conditions to meet expectations. I have glorified war, grossly simplified complicated events, and grossly complicated simple events. . . . And now it is time for someone else to do it.

Editors come and go, but writers have to live with themselves forever. If you're a writer, remember that your long-term integrity is more important than any editor's short-term needs. Think long, and try not to lose discretion.

KEVIN MCKEAN, a senior editor at *Money* magazine, began his career as a general-assignment reporter and night rewrite-man for the Associated Press in Denver and New Orleans. He moved to the AP's New York bureau as a senior science writer, "happily chasing after many of the major science stories of the day," including Three Mile Island, the eruption of Mount St. Helens and the cancer treatment of the Shah of Iran. In 1981 he joined the newly launched science magazine *Discover* as a writer and senior editor, covering subjects ranging from ancient apes to the end of the universe. Upon the sale of that magazine he moved to *Money*, where he now specializes as a writer and editor on stories about personal finance. He continues to be involved in science and medicine as a freelance writer. He was series science editor for the three-hour PBS-TV special, *Living Against the Odds*, which dealt with elements of risk in everyday life. He lives in New York with his wife, Pamela, and their daughter, Kyle.

3

KEVIN MCKEAN

SCIENCE, TECHNOLOGY AND MEDICINE

What does the term "regression to the mean" mean to you? Probably not much, unless you know something about statistics. And if I gave you a textbook definition you'd probably stop listening right now. But if you'll stick with me at least through the following excerpt you may come away with an insight into regression that changes how you view everyday events. It's from an article I wrote for *Discover* magazine about the work of two psychologists named Amos Tversky and Daniel Kahneman. They study the innate logic—and illogic—of the human mind. This excerpt describes an incident that happened to Kahneman while he was teaching Air Force flight instructors about the psychology of training. He begins by citing animal studies, some done with pigeons, which show that reward is a more effective teaching tool than punishment.

Suddenly one of the flight instructors, barely waiting for Kahneman to finish, blurted out: "With respect, sir, what you are saying is literally for the birds. I've often praised people warmly for beautifully executed maneuvers, and the next time they almost always do worse. And I've screamed at them for badly executed maneuvers, and by and large the next time they improve. Don't tell me that reward works and punishment doesn't. My experience contradicts it." The other flight instructors agreed.

The challenge left Kahneman momentarily speechless. "I suddenly realized," he says "that this was an example of the statistical principle of regression to the mean, and that nobody else had ever seen this before. It was one of the most exciting moments of my career."

Regression to the mean, as Kahneman told the pilots, was the notion established by the English gentleman-scientist Sir Francis Galton (1822–1911), that in any series of random events clustering around an average, or mean, an extraordinary event was most likely to be followed—just by luck of the draw—by a more ordinary event. Thus, very tall fathers tend to have slightly shorter sons, and very short fathers somewhat taller ones.

Although regression is usually discussed in narrow statistical terms, it affects virtually every series of events that is to some degree random. And since there's almost nothing in life that isn't at least partly a matter of chance, regression shows up in a wide variety of unlikely places. It helps explain why brilliant wives tend to have slightly duller husbands, great movies have disappointing sequels, and disastrous presidents have better successors. The student pilots, Kahneman explained, were improving their skills so slowly that the difference in performance from one maneuver to the next was largely a matter of luck. Regression dictated that a student who made a perfect three-point landing today would make a bumpier one tomorrow, regardless of praise or blame. But the flight instructors, failing to realize this, had underestimated the effectiveness of reward and overestimated the effectiveness of punishment.

Kahneman realized that what had been true of the student pilots would also be true of dancers learning to pirouette, chefs learning to bake bread, salesmen learning to close a deal and children learning to obey. "By regression alone," he and Tversky later wrote, "behavior is most likely to improve after punishment and to deteriorate after reward. Consequently . . . one is most often rewarded for punishing others and most often punished for rewarding them."

My reason for reading you this passage is not to convince you of the importance of regression but to make a point about writing: that it's possible to describe even dry and complicated subjects, like regression, in a clear and accessible and at least somewhat entertaining way.

That's what I want to talk to you about: how to make highly specialized subjects accessible to readers. I've brought along some examples that illustrate principles I've followed in my own career as a science writer. All of them are from magazine-length articles about science or medicine. But the techniques could apply to any writing where the challenge is to convey a body of arcane and complex technical information. It could be a legal brief, or an engineering report, or an instruction manual, or a financial prospectus. In my present job as a senior editor at *Money* magazine I use the same techniques to explain complex issues of personal finance.

In technical writing, all the usual writer's tools are important: style, narrative, dialogue, anecdote and so forth. But one element supersedes all the rest: clarity. A piece of technical writing that explains its subject clearly but fails in every other literary respect will still outshine an elegant article whose meaning is obscure. Technical writing exists to convey information. All other aspects of the craft must serve that end.

Science writing is a particularly satisfying form of technical writing because the canvas is so rich and broad. Over the years I've had the enjoyment of writing about artificial hearts and biological computers, long-extinct ancestors and future cataclysms, dinosaurs and racehorses, blue-green algae and black holes. Many experts who study these phenomena are gifted storytellers; they can describe their own research more eloquently than I ever could. But most of them—who knows, perhaps because of regression to the mean—are indifferent communicators. For them a good technical writer is a valuable ally: an interpreter, explicator, popularizer and historian. And today, with science and technology increasingly shaping our lives, it's important for writers to do the job well.

But it's not easy. Readers nowadays are incredibly demanding. They have too many competing sources of information—from print and broadcast media to software and, God help us, "virtual reality"—to waste their time on sloppy or self-indulgent writing. They expect you to tell them exactly as much as they need to know, and no more. Their patience is short.

Therefore your first job is to decide how much technical information you can afford to include. Not that science or medicine is inherently boring; most scientific discoveries are very exciting, once you know enough background to understand their implications. The discoverer, of course, knows this background thoroughly; he or she has probably spent a lifetime studying it. The reader, on the other hand (and often the writer too), is apt to be technologically naive. He may have never heard of the topic. Or if he's a specialist of some kind—a doctor reading about medicine, or a lawyer about law—he may know a lot about the subject in general but little about the new discovery. In any case, he doesn't know as much as the expert who made the discovery. So the question you as a writer must ask yourself is: "How much of what the expert knows do I have to learn, and tell, to make the work intelligible to other people?"

In struggling with this problem I've found it helpful to think of the writer as constructing a bridge between what the reader knows and what the expert knows. Both of them share a certain foundation of simple scientific knowledge, learned in school and gleaned from popular culture. They both took algebra in high school, dissected a frog in biology class, read about cloning in the newspaper, and so forth. You might picture that shared foundation of knowledge this way:

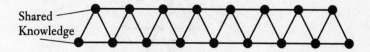

Shared
Knowledge

But while the average reader's scientific knowledge stops there, the expert proceeds to build on that foundation in college, graduate school and years of professional work. He or she amasses a growing body of ever more specialized information about a particular field—for example, human genetics and the cloning of genes—that you might picture like this:

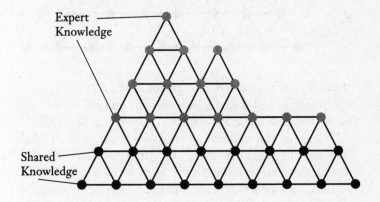

Expert
Knowledge

Shared
Knowledge

Eventually the expert's knowledge leads to an important discovery. Maybe she clones the gene whose malfunction causes some important disease, pointing the way to new treatments. You, the writer, want to describe that discovery—which, in our diagram, might appear like the figure on the next page.

Your job is to look for a simple path that will connect what the reader already knows with what the expert has found. If you were writing a textbook you might fill in the entire triangle. But as a magazine or newspaper writer you have to get the job done much faster. You need to find two or three funda-

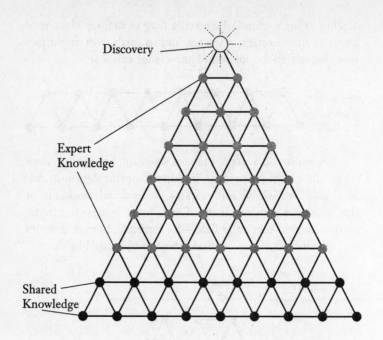

mental facts that can serve as stepping-stones across this river of information and define a path that you and the reader can follow. The path might look like the figure on the next page.

Here's an example from a booklet I wrote, called "The Frontiers of Cancer Research," for Memorial Sloan-Kettering Cancer Center in New York. It's organized into a series of chapters, each of which deals with one aspect of current scientific investigation. The passages I'm going to read to you explore the notion that cancer is essentially a disruption of normal growth. To develop that idea I proceed from a simple fact—a fact known to most of us—about how life begins:

> At its moment of conception, any multi-celled creature—be it a fish, fly or person—consists of just a single cell. But this state of unity does not last long. Within hours, usually, the one cell divides into two. Then the two become four; the four, eight; the eight, sixteen; and so on.
>
> The plan for this intricate development lies in the genes

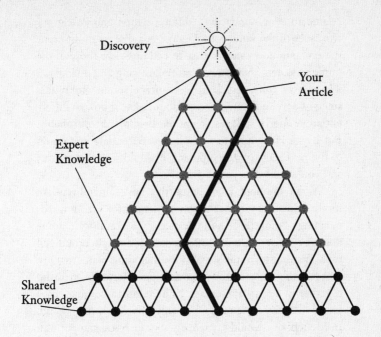

that the creature inherits from its mother and father. At first the instructions for all cells seem to be identical. But soon, in a process that scientists call *differentiation*, individual cells begin to play different roles. As early as the fifth day in the human embryo, for example, the cells that give rise to the embryo can be distinguished from those that will create the placenta that connects it to the womb. By the third week the forerunners of skin, bone and nerve cells have differentiated and begun to follow their own unique parts of the master growth plan. By adulthood, virtually all cells have differentiated into mature types that divide slowly, if at all.

Having introduced the concept that cells grow and differentiate according to a controlled plan, the chapter proceeds to argue that cancer occurs when that control fails:

"For me," says Dr. François Jacob of the Pasteur Institute in Paris, a 1965 Nobel Prize winner for discoveries related to gene regulation, "differentiation and cancer are two faces of the same coin. Cancer is a disease of differentiation, and most cancers arise in cell lines like those of the immune system that are constantly growing and dividing.... The cancer cell is stuck in some precursor or embryonic stage of development. The cell doesn't know how to differentiate properly, so it just keeps on dividing uncontrollably. But if you knew how to force it to differentiate and go on to the next stage of development, it would stop this growth and you would cure your cancer."

As an example Jacob cites the unusual embryo-like tumor known as teratocarcinoma. Named for Greek words meaning "monster" and "cancer," a teratocarcinoma doesn't consist—as most tumors do—of a single errant cell type. Instead, it's a jumble of cells, including many that are recognizably normal nerve, muscle or other cells, growing together in a misshapen mass. "The teratocarcinoma," says Jacob, "is a cell gone mad—but only transiently mad. Wild. In French, one would say *sauvage*, because you can put him back in society, so to speak, and reeducate him, and he will stop being a cancer. By this I mean that if you inject the teratocarcinoma cell into an embryo it will stop being cancerous and will participate in the confection of an animal. It's the equivalent of an early embryonic cell which, for some reason, has escaped normal growth control. By placing it back in the embryo you force it to be regulated again."

With cancer and differentiation now firmly linked, I can go on to the marvel I've been aiming for all along—the discovery of chemicals that "reeducate" cancer cells by forcing them to differentiate, mature and stop dividing. Many such chemicals exist. Most are effective only in the lab, but a few have become important in the treatment of human cancer.

But the chapter doesn't end there. Having raised the notion that each generation begets the next by passing along a template contained in the genes, my story pauses to quote a scientist who makes a philosophical point about this fact.

"What fascinates me," observes Dr. Gunter Blobel of Rockefeller University, "is the continuity of life. If you think about your father and mother, and then about their fathers and mothers, and their fathers and mothers, and so on back into time, eventually you will get to somebody who was a frog. Then to somebody who was a single cell. And this life has gone on uninterruptedly for more than three billion years on earth. So as we stand here we are part of a continuous lineage that goes back three billion years.

"This is a tremendous thing that we don't realize in our everyday life, this fantastic continuity. What does it mean? How long will it last? Each of us is related to the entire world and all of the people and animals and plants in it. Yet we haven't translated this idea into ethics or politics. Perhaps if we did, we would be more considerate and humane."

From the differentiation of cells to cancer treatment to the ethical lessons of evolution—all built in a series of steps on the simple foundation of a single-celled embryo.

But because each step involves something of a leap, you need some way to make the stepping-stones plainly visible. Here your best weapons often are analogy and metaphor. In those passages, for example, Dr. Jacob compares a teratocarcinoma cell to a wild man, or *sauvage*, tamed by reeducation. For many readers this conjures up visions of a Tarzan-like character—a powerful image that contains a wealth of information without having to spell it out. The metaphor implies, among other things, that the teratocarcinoma cell is more primitive than normal cells (true), that it is vigorous and active but often inappropriately so (also true), and that by coming into contact with more "civilized" cells it can reform its behavior and rejoin polite society (also true, though nobody knows whether the teratocarcinoma pines, as Tarzan did, for its jungle existence).

A vivid metaphor helps everybody—the reader, the writer and the scientist. Take the case of "receptors." By the 1970s it had become clear that many biologically active substances, such as hormones and certain drugs, exert their influence by attaching themselves to the surface of particular cells. The attachment is by no means haphazard; the target cell must display a molecule to which the hormone will bind. These binding molecules are incredibly discriminating; the insulin-binding molecule, for instance, will accept only insulin or its close chemical relatives. Thus scientists came to call these molecules "receptors"—the insulin receptor, the opiate receptor, etc.

In describing these receptors, scientists often fell back on the analogy of a lock and key. The receptor was like a lock, they said, and the hormone was like a key that fit the lock. The image was descriptive, but it also proved to be prophetic. Today, scientists believe that the binding occurs because the receptor assumes a shape that is complementary to that of the hormone, just as the teeth on a key complement the tumblers of a lock. Where the receptor has a negatively charged hollow, the hormone has a positively charged knob, and vice versa, so that electrical attraction tends to cleave them together. Furthermore, just as turning a key engages an internal mechanism to unlatch a door, the binding of the hormone seems to bend the receptor in such a way that its tail, which projects down into the cell, sets off a chemical cascade that achieves the hormone's effect.

But metaphors must be used with caution. They can also lead you astray, as the following excerpt from my Memorial Sloan-Kettering book shows. The story was told to me by Dr. Arthur Kornberg of Stanford University, a Nobel Prize winner who has spent his life studying how cells make copies of DNA, the genetic material that must be duplicated each time a cell divides:

> The duplicating machinery consists of a series of specialized enzymes, the proteins that carry out chemical reactions in a cell. The first of these twists the DNA into a tight circle, prying apart its double helix. A second enzyme slips into the cleavage and opens it wider. Then a dozen or more enzymes collect to prime the DNA, lay down a new copy, proofread their work for errors and untwist any parts that get twisted.

In his mental picture of this, Kornberg used to imagine a locomotive barreling down the DNA tracks. He even worked out fanciful metaphors in which one enzyme was the cow-catcher, clearing the tracks; another the engine, turning the wheels, and so forth. But then he ran into one of those rude shocks that make scrap metal of such picturesque thinking: "When we examined the parts of the 'locomotive' separately we found that two of them went one way down the track while the other two went in the opposite direction. And of course that's no way to run a railroad!" Now Kornberg conceives of the replicating machinery as stationary, pulling the DNA through it like a sewing machine pulling fabric.

But finally what makes a story entertaining is its human dimension. The charm of the passage I just read lies in Kornberg's self-deprecating humor. We get the sense of a serious and dedicated person who still appreciates a good joke, even if it's on himself.

Throughout scientific and technical writing, it's people who pull the reader along, just as Kornberg's enzymes pull the DNA through their clutches. Readers are people, after all; they like to read about other people—their achievements and failures, their hopes and dreams. That's why, whenever I interview a scientist—or anyone, for that matter—I try to find out what moves him or her about the work. I ask questions like: How did you first get interested in this subject? What events in your life prepared you for your discovery? How did you feel when you failed, or succeeded? My aim is to discover the answers to even larger metaphysical questions—things like: What does it feel like to be you? And how does the experience of being you shed light on the mystery of what it feels like to be me?

Often those questions help me to clarify the factors that drive the scientist—which inevitably makes his or her story more interesting. In 1982, for *Discover*, I wrote a profile of E. O. Wilson, the Harvard sociobiologist. During the 1970s Wilson had stirred faculty and student criticism by proposing that much of human behavior might be genetically programmed. He said, for instance, that there may be genes for altruism, or promiscuity, or male dominance, or fear of strangers. His critics, many from the political left, accused him of providing excuses for racism, sexism and social oppression. But in fact Wilson's ideas had grown out of years of observing animals whose behavior is clearly under some degree of genetic control, ranging from ants (his specialty) to apes and monkeys. His heresy had been to propose that we human beings are not really so different from these creatures and that our society, like theirs, evolves to "fit" its environment, much as individual organisms do. My article opened with an epigraph from Albert Camus—a passage that Wilson was particularly fond of:

> *A man's work is nothing but the slow trek to rediscover, through the detours of art, those two or three great and simple images in whose presence his heart first opened.*
>
> *—Albert Camus*

In the summer of 1939 two small boys carrying homemade butterfly nets made their way across a hillside in the narrow wilderness of Rock Creek Park in Washington, D.C. Noticing a rotting tree stump, one of them paused to tear loose a chunk of wood. Suddenly hordes of tiny yellow insects gushed from the hole, and an odor of citronella, like the scent of mosquito-repellent candles, rose from the ground.

The boys had disturbed a colony of ants—*Acanthomyops*, to be exact, a common North American genus, although neither of them knew it at the time. "They were so brilliantly colored and exquisite in design," recalls Edward Osborne Wilson, Jr., "and there were so many of them living in a large society. It made me wonder what they were doing down there, how far they went into the soil, how they fit into their environment." Wilson went on to become a world-famous expert on ants. He proved, among other things, that the citronella smell was an alarm substance given off by *Acanthomyops* when attacked. But he never forgot the notion that any society—however complex—must somehow "fit" into its environment, and this idea was destined to make him one of the world's most controversial scientists.

The trick in science writing is to mix the human story with the science story so cleverly that the reader never tires of either. The easiest way is to alternate one with the other: a little science, a little human interest, and so forth. A typical example is my earlier passage about regression to the mean and its lessons about punishment and reward. It opens with a human incident (a classroom of flight instructors), wanders off briefly into mathematics, and then circles back to everyday experiences we can all identify with: children learning to obey, or salesmen learning how to close a deal. The entire story is constructed as a series of such passages, each one mixing science and humanity in some proportion. Walter Sullivan of *The New York Times*, one of the deans of American science reporters, is a master of that strategy. It's like spoonfeeding the reader vanilla-chocolate-fudge ice cream. Since you don't know which flavor he likes best, vanilla or chocolate, you feed him alternating spoonfuls. You hope he'll stay with you through the spoonfuls he doesn't like so as to catch more of his favorite flavor.

Even when the human element turns out to be disappointing it can sometimes be made to work. A few years ago I was writing a story about emergency rescue procedures in Seattle. Its point was that the city's rescue system is among the world's finest and saves many lives. To dramatize the point I focused on one person who had been saved, a city official named Ronald Tegard, who had a heart attack.

My intention was to interview Mr. Tegard and all the people who cooperated to save him. By chance, however, I reached Mr. Tegard last, and when I finally heard his side of the story my spirits sank. I don't know exactly what I had expected—something with lots of passion and drama, I suppose. After all, the man had died and been brought back to life. But Mr. Tegard turned out to be such a matter-of-fact person that the incident hadn't bothered him much. Sure, the heart attack was a defining event in his life. Yet to hear him describe it you'd think he was talking about having a flat tire.

Then I realized that this lack of emotion made his story better. In Seattle, apparently, emergency rescue had become so sophisticated that death itself could be a non-event. Here's how the story began:

Of all the nights in Ronald D. Tegard's life, one that will stick in his mind forever is the night he died.

Not that the death itself was particularly memorable. His life history didn't flash before his eyes. He didn't have an out-of-body experience, or see spirits in a blinding light, or have any of the other stock encounters of popular mythology about that great beyond. In fact, he doesn't remember being dead at all. What he recalls are the events just before and after.

"It was November 10th, 1989," says Mr. Tegard, 55, a staff assistant to the personnel director of the city of Seattle. "I had gone to the health club for my regular Friday night workout. Somebody was using the Nautilus machine, so I went to the cardiovascular room and did an easygoing 15 minutes on the stair machine to kill time. After that I wandered over by the water fountain and took a cup of water. Suddenly I felt dizzy and started looking for a place to go down. I don't remember hitting the floor."

What had happened to Mr. Tegard is something that befalls hundreds of thousands of Americans each year. Without warning, his heart had degenerated into an abnormal rhythm—in his case, an aimless quivering called fibrillation. His breathing stopped; his pulse vanished; his brain ceased to function; he turned blue. In a word, he was dead.

But fortunately for Mr. Tegard, he had suffered his cardiac arrest in a city with perhaps the best emergency rescue system in the country. Seattle's citizens are its first line of defense. One in three of them—including Judy Sheridan, who heard Mr. Tegard thump to the floor—are trained in cardiopulmonary resuscitation. "I thought he'd had a seizure," recalls Mrs. Sheridan, a fourth-grade teacher and mother of six. "But another club member found he didn't have any pulse. So that man worked on his chest and I worked on his mouth while my 12-year-old son Ryan ran to call 911. It was scary. But once I started, everything I had learned in CPR class came back to me."

By that time, firefighters were racing to the health club with a defibrillator, the shock device used to jump-start a stalled heart. "After the second jolt his pulse came back," says rescue worker Ron Calender. Fire Captain Mike McIntyre recalls, "When we got there, the guy seemed dead. But by the time they put in the breathing tube he was gagging, which is actually a good sign."

Mr. Tegard remembers waking up in the ambulance. "I recognized where I was," he says, "but they had a tube down my throat so I couldn't make a sound. "The next thing I remember is being in the intensive care unit, surrounded by wires and tubes, with my 18-year-old daughter Dixi there. We lost her mother to cancer just four years ago, and I'm the only family she's got, so she was pretty scared. But once she realized I was basically okay, she was relieved."

Eleven days later, surgeons operated on Mr. Tegard to restore blood flow to his heart. The following week he went home. The following month he and Dixi took the trip to Hawaii they had been planning. And today, back at work full-time and exercising moderately three times a week, Mr. Tegard feels almost as fit as he did before he died. "It was just an incident that happened, and that's that," he says. "You try to forget it."

One final word. Learning to write, like learning any skill, is easier with good instruction, and I hope this class will help you improve your writing. But teaching only communicates those aspects of a craft that can be codified, boiled down to concepts and expressed in words. Real craftsmanship is richer than that. It involves many things that you can learn only by doing them. So the best way to improve your writing is to write often. Practice is the best teacher of all.

WILLIAM ZINSSER • I had asked Kevin McKean to talk to our class mainly out of his long experience as a science writer, because one of the hardest and most important jobs that journalists are routinely given is to make complex technical subjects clear. But by then McKean was a senior editor of *Money* magazine, an expert at clarifying the no less complex issues of personal finance, and during the class he detoured into that world to show us that the process of demystifying money is little different from the process of writing about science and medicine.

"Even stories about some simple aspect of finance," he said, "have the same dramatic elements, the same structure and hooks, as any other piece of writing, including good fiction." Just as he had said that in science "the trick is to mix the human story with the science story so cleverly that the reader never tires of either," in personal finance the solution comes down to finding a human narrative somewhere in the tangle of facts and figures, preferably one that has mystery, suspense and that old movie standby—a chase. He cited an article he had edited for *Money* called "When It Pays to Swap Your Mortgage"—hardly a tale, one would think, to stir the blood. Yet as he read that story aloud we were as attentive as if we had been sitting around a campfire. How would the chase come out? Would the cavalry—the refinanced mortgage—get there in time to save the situation?

McKean said he always tries to remember a line from *All the President's Men*, the movie about Watergate. "Woodward and Bernstein are stuck," he recalled, "and 'Deep Throat' tells them, 'Follow the money, follow the money.' My maxim is: If you follow the money flow of people's lives you'll find out where their hearts are. Our magazine did a profile of a man who never went to college and didn't think college was something a parent owed his child. He had a good blue-collar job. He said, 'I love my kids, but I don't want to pay for their education. If they want to go to college they're going to have to pay for it themselves.'

"But when we got the family's tax returns and looked at their budget, there was money missing. The income and the outgo weren't adding up, by several thousands of dollars, in a family whose total budget was around $40,000. So we went back to them, and they kept trying to explain it away, and we kept going back and kept going back, and finally we discovered that the wife was secretly siphoning off the money to give it to the kids on the side to help them meet their college expenses. She begged us not to put it in the story, and we didn't, and maybe we failed ethically as journalists for not including it. But it's a wonderful example of 'Follow the money and you'll find out where their hearts are.'

"I should add that whenever we met with the husband and the wife to discuss their budget he would say, 'We think our kids should make it on their own,' and she would always say, 'Yes, yes, I agree.'"

CORBY KUMMER has been senior editor of *The Atlantic Monthly* since 1981, responsible for many of its nonfiction pieces, including humor and articles on politics and the arts. He writes regularly on food and travel for the *Atlantic* and other magazines, including *Travel Holiday, Condé Nast Traveler, The New York Times Magazine, Mirabella, Eating Well, BarGiornale* and the *Journal of Gastronomy*. His *Atlantic* cover story on pasta and a subsequent series on coffee drew wide attention, and he is now writing a book on buying and brewing coffee.

4

CORBY KUMMER

EDITORS AND WRITERS

Just an hour ago I ran into a former classmate, Paul Rudnick, who is now a successful humorist and playwright, and I mentioned that I was going to talk to you about the relationship between writer and editor. "Handcuffs," he said. He's right. It does start with initial distrust on the part of the writer, who has probably been mauled and manhandled so often by places like *The New York Times Magazine*, where editors just want to get their paws all over his copy and don't tell him what's happening, that most writers take a very wary stance.

There's a good writer, a real pro, named Peter Hellman, who writes for *New York* and many other magazines. I was once given a piece of his to edit, and five minutes after we met he said, at the first very mild suggestion I made, "Don't fuck with my copy." He's actually a sweetheart, but he was expecting the worst. And in fact, as a writer you always have to. Writers don't like having their words changed. Ultimately, if an editor does his work properly, writers are grateful; anybody smart is pleased to be edited well. But it's painful while it's happening.

My first editing job was at a magazine called *Quest*, where we were a small and close staff. I was very cocky, and I would get these pieces and think: I know how to write this better. I would sit down and rewrite an article to make it—I thought—faster and livelier. Then I'd put it into type and send the galleys to the writer and say, "If you have any changes, call," thinking that of course he or she would be so pleased to see what a nice job I had done, making the piece better. One writer, Frank Rose, called back and slowly but surely restored every word in his story. We went over it line by line, and I thought: Is this some kind of conspiracy? I would say, "Gee, I don't know if I like that sentence." And he would say, "But that's what I wrote; this *isn't* what I wrote."

When I got to the *Atlantic* I was firmly told that rewriting is the amateur way of editing. You never rewrite if you can avoid it. You have to give the writer his or her own voice. You have to work within the authors' prose as much as you possibly can. You tighten, and you make *them* do the work—whatever rewriting is necessary—because their name goes on it. Your goal is to be a good surgeon who can open things up and change the order around—change the internal organs but sew up the body and not show the scars; it's still a working body.

In those first years at the *Atlantic* I was so young that to meet writers in person was a liability. I made sure to do everything over the phone, which is always more efficient—you can just concentrate on the words. I remember I was given a piece by George Kennan, who is my boss's hero. He said, "This is one of the last grand old men—you must have a very light touch with him." Well, I read his article and I thought: He's really saying everything twice. I want to cut this substantially. And I did. Over the phone I asked Kennan these endless questions, and every time we talked he nearly hung up on me every few minutes. It was an ordeal. Yet he didn't flat-out reject any of it, because I wasn't rewriting him.

I was trying to cut the piece and make it tighter. Later I heard that he told his agent, "That young man gave me as much trouble as *The New Yorker*." My boss, Bill Whitworth, was delighted. He told the agent, "That's what he's supposed to do." So no matter how important the writer is, you should work on his piece as hard as you would on any article. But you have to be very respectful. You have to be careful to maintain the writer's tone and voice.

In the old days before computers, editors used scissors and paste; I would literally cut up pieces and put them in a different order. Even with new technology, what I do is still pretty primitive. How I start, very often, especially with a long piece, is to outline it, because not all writers are used to writing more than 1,500 or 2,000 words. But at the *Atlantic* our average piece is 3,500 words—if we're lucky. In the middle of the magazine the articles run anywhere from 5,000 to 15,000 words. It's surprising how many writers write without an outline. What I often have to do is to make a list of all the topics in the piece and then figure out a sensible outline for them and put them together in some logical sequence. Mainly I try to clarify—to make the writer clarify.

Also, I'm a generalist; I am not an expert on anything. If *I* can follow a piece, anybody can. So I'm editing for the curious, well-educated but not specialist reader. I never pretend to be a specialist. At the *Atlantic*, as you can imagine, our staple is public-affairs pieces, so if I don't understand something about how a bill gets passed, or about how a lobbyist operates, or about some scientific issue, I have to ask enough questions and ask the writer for inserts until I *can* understand it.

One master of this art is the radio interviewer Terry Gross. She gets the most interesting people in politics and entertainment on her show, and she'll never hesitate to ask the question that reveals that she is not in the know. That infinitely helps the listener. Terry Gross never shies from asking the specialist a question that implies, "We're not pals together on the sophisticated side of this velvet rope."

In my own work as a writer I try to maintain that general-ist's approach, because I have a specialty, which is food, and I'm writing for a magazine, the *Atlantic*, whose readers, I assume, basically couldn't care less about food. I have to explain what kneading bread means, for example. I have to try to keep the readers engaged and to make the subject entertaining. So by the same principle, a lot of editing is asking questions.

One easy and manipulative way of opening a conversation with a writer is to ask him what he wants his bio to say—the few sentences that explain his credentials. It's such unabashed pandering to the writer's ego, but it usually works. Once you start asking real questions you often have to ask the same thing many times. Recently I've been working on a very long piece about population—why we should dread population growth, or maybe why we shouldn't—and I've already received a rewrite on the last third of the piece. I asked the author, "What are we going to be left with at the end of this piece? Do we have to worry about the future or not?" He kept hedging, and I kept asking what his real opinion was. Finally he said that over the last thousand years the human race has found a way out of every tight spot and we're proba-bly going to find ways out of this one that we can't imagine right now, so let's not get too worked up. That's a typical *Atlantic* solution: "Let's be sensible and not alarmist." But it was hard to get an opinion out of him. Writers are often so close to their material that it's hard for them to pull together—out of all this information—what's important to leave with the reader. The editor's responsibility is to figure out what finally is the point of the story and why the maga-zine is running it.

Without a clear idea of this, things can go wrong for everybody. Not long ago I wrote a food piece about freeze-drying, for a camping magazine. They called me out of the blue—I'm the least likely person; I always want to be near a 24-hour newsstand where you can get coffee and bagels. But I often write about food technology, and this editor wanted something about technological processes: How does food for campers wind up in these pellets? So I collected all sorts of information about the technology and wrote the article, and it turned out that the *other* editors of the magazine wanted to know how you make the food better on the trail and what it tastes like. Unfortunately, when I tried it I couldn't eat it; the stuff really is appalling. The other thing is, I didn't *go* on the trail, and they wanted anecdotes. They gave me the names of some campers to interview, and when I called those people they said they either hated freeze-dried food or they loved it; it was impossible to get a reason out of them. The interviews didn't give me what I needed, and I hadn't known I would need that kind of material when I took the assignment.

The point is twofold. As a writer I don't like being spoken to in two voices. In this case, different editors at the camping magazine wanted different stories. I wrote what I had been asked to write, and it was jarring to find out that something else was wanted. Although the request made sense, I resented having the rules changed on me. That was the famous practice at *The New York Times Magazine*, where editors would call and say, "I like this, and I agree this should be the tone of the piece, but *they* say it's got to be another way."

The second point of the story is that as an editor I'm lucky to work at a magazine where we speak with one voice. I can decide what I want to do with the piece I'm editing. I get suggestions from my colleagues on what it might need, but I'm not obliged to take them. I can overrule my boss, and I do so regularly, mostly because he has done only a fast reading of the piece, whereas I'm closely in tune with it and I want to see that it honors the author's intentions and our own aims. The *Times Magazine* once interviewed me for a job as an editor, and at the end I said to them, "Do I get final control over the piece? Can I overrule you?" They looked at each other and laughed. They said, "That's not how it works here."

*   *   *

In general, there are two kinds of magazine styles in this matter of assigning articles. *The New York Times Magazine*, for example, is proud to say that it generates 75 to 80 percent of the ideas for its pieces. But at *The New Yorker*—at least at the old *New Yorker*—the classic principle is that the author has to be really impassioned about a subject. I remember saying to Bill Whitworth when I first came to the *Atlantic*, "Let's get X to write about Y," because at my previous job, at *Quest*, we commissioned a lot of pieces, and that was fun. But Bill said that when a magazine dreams up the idea and asks a writer to do it, usually neither of them is completely pleased. The result is always a little different from what the magazine expected and a little different from what the writer wanted to do. It's better for the writer to want to write the piece and to be in a position to know how to go out and research it.

At the *Atlantic* the process starts with a letter from the writer setting out his or her intentions, saying, "Here's why I want to write this piece." I'll send the letter along to my boss, and generally he'll show it to one other editor; it's a tiny staff. Between my boss and the other editor they'll say, "Yes, this is interesting. What we *really* want to hear about is this." So then I'll call the writer and say, "Here's what we'd like, in this many words. You don't have to do a lot of interviews (or you *do* have to do a lot of interviews). Here's what we're hoping for." The more specific you are at the outset, the happier everyone will be with the result. You don't suddenly change the rules, as the camping magazine did with me.

As an editor, when you're working with a writer and have his trust, it's a collaboration. At that point it's interesting how reliant the writer becomes on you. You can never pull rank, but there's something of the father confessor in the relationship. That's a dramatic way of putting it, but it applies to different authors to different degrees. You, the editor, become an authority figure to your writers because you're telling them what to do. These are things they care a lot about and feel very strongly about—things they have put a part of themselves into. And you're asking them to change, to clarify, to sharpen. So you can't turn it into something lighthearted or frivolous, because they've come to rely on you for direction.

I take very seriously my relationship with writers, and many of them are friends. But you befriend a writer in a different way from the way you befriend a friend. As a writer I get mistreated by magazines regularly, so I'm sympathetic. But as an editor I can't complain to writers about that, because it's not what they want to hear; it's also not pertinent. My job is to present writers in the best possible way—to try to get them to write as well and as clearly as they can.

Often, of course, when you work with writers, you're convinced that something should be changed and they're equally insistent that it should stay the way it is. How does that get resolved? I try to make them think they thought of the change themselves. You ask certain questions and you make certain suggestions, but not very strongly. You do it in a vague way that you hope will lead them to a specific point you want, so they then think it's what *they* wanted. That's the ideal. It's not always easy to do.

Recently I've had a very satisfying collaboration with David Schiff, a professor of music at Reed College, who had previously written a wonderful cover story for us on Leonard Bernstein. He's the rare writer who gives you more than you asked for, taking your suggestions and going farther than you were even able to imagine when you sketched out what you wanted—something that's so gratifying it can be exhilarating.

But with this new article of his, which was about a music class he taught on music composed since 1945, I was in the dark. I couldn't make head or tail of the first half—a discussion of how hard it is for any kind of experimental music to get a performance on FM radio. Evidently FM classical music stations are more commercially driven than those high-minded stations make themselves out to be. But when the writer got into the progress of the class itself, and how his students surprised him with their stubborn insistence on judging a composition—whatever its style—by whether they sensed that the composer was authentic or phony, I became involved and interested in the story.

I told him that in the first part of the piece I had the feeling he was pacing in front of a blackboard, talking fluently and trying hard—and noticeably—to hit on a subject for his lecture. I can't always be that frank with a writer. Often you need to cite some internal situation at your magazine—space limitations or deadline problems—to force a writer to focus on his material and agree to cuts you think are essential to strengthening the piece. As with friends, frankness is a luxury you earn slowly and can't abuse—but it sure makes things move faster. In this case the writer told me he had the same feeling about his article. That was the breakthrough. Then he and I could get down to talking about what should stay and what should go.

In three days he rewrote his draft almost completely, paying attention to transitions and making everything seem to have a natural place. I wasn't crazy about all the points he wanted to keep in, but the essay had a clear structure and didn't repeat itself, and after that I had to shut up. In fact, I liked most of it. But you don't have to like the subject or the writer's point of view. You have to help the piece make sense on its own terms and to maintain its individual tone.

Although it's important to keep the writer's voice, even when you don't like it (which happens to me a lot), I don't hesitate to kill darlings. I'm sure you've heard that axiom of good writing—you must "murder your darlings," the phrases you really love. My own darlings are killed frequently. Sometimes I fight to keep them in, and later I almost always regret it. Last night I was rereading some pieces I wrote about coffee, because I'm now writing a book on that subject. I cringed when I came upon two or three lines I had fought to keep. I thought they were so clever at the time; now I thought, yuck, I'm sorry that stayed. Because usually what you think is delicious isn't. It's better off gone.

My boss once showed me an edit of an *Atlantic* piece that

a *New Yorker* editor named Gardner Botsford did for him, as a demonstration. I was in awe of what he accomplished. He made small deletions, or just changed a word or two in every sentence, which made it flow much better. That to me is the most brilliant editing—being able to condense and tighten almost everything.

WILLIAM ZINSSER • Corby Kummer's parting salute to Gardner Botsford couldn't help reminding me of Gardner Botsford's parting salute to William Shawn, the near-mythical
editor of *The New Yorker*, who died in the autumn of 1992. In
its issue of Dec. 28, 1992/Jan. 4, 1993, *The New Yorker* ran a
folio of remembrances by 32 of its longtime writers and
artists, each of whom, it said, "felt that he or she had enjoyed
a special and irreplaceable relationship with the man." Of all
those memoirs, Botsford's was the one I most enjoyed and
admired—the perfect epilogue, I think, to Kummer's chapter
and his innate respect for the idea that a good editor's work
should be unseen and unsung.

Botsford begins by recalling that *The New Yorker*'s
founder, Harold Ross, had two favorite apothegms: "No
monkey business with the girls in the office" and "Any editor
worth a damn has to take a vow of anonymity." He goes on to
say:

> It may be that William Shawn carried anonymity one
> veil too far, but what appeared to be an endearing eccen-
> tricity in the modern workaday world was an invaluable
> tool in the world of manuscripts. Ross's dictum had been
> wrung from him during the war, when the draft carried off
> every fact editor but Ross himself and Shawn, and he had
> tried to turn undrafted writers into makeshift editors. The
> experiment was soon abandoned; the writers in wolf's
> clothing enraged their fellows to the point of insurrection
> by rewriting everything handed to them and imprinting
> their own style and tone on the copy.
>
> Shawn was nothing like that. He would take a failed
> text, saw it up into a dozen chunks, excise the vacant mus-
> ings, straighten out the thinking, fix the grammar, oil the

transitions, and put it back together as an acceptable piece of work—all without leaving a trace of his presence. Only the writer knew that Shawn had been there, and the writer wasn't likely to tell. When I started work as an editor, in 1945, Shawn gave me as a manual of instruction a manuscript he had edited, by a writer now long and deservedly forgotten. The thing was a revelation. Every page of the manuscript was black with Shawn's crabbed little corrections and transpositions, and the margins were littered with requests for more facts or better explanations. He had, it became clear, completely rewritten the piece— but always carefully using the lame writer's own language and constructions. What was astonishing was that by the time the job was done Shawn himself had vanished. There was nobody left but the writer—but now a writer who had a competent piece to offer.

JANE MAYER began covering politics, entertainment, and social issues and trends in 1981 for *The Wall Street Journal*, where she was a senior writer assigned to the front page. She was the paper's White House correspondent from 1984 to 1987, when she took a leave of absence to write a book, with Doyle McManus, about the Reagan administration's involvement in the Iran-Contra affair. The book, *Landslide: The Unmaking of the President* (Houghton Mifflin, 1988), became a national best-seller.

After returning to the paper to cover such stories as the Gulf War and the fall of the Berlin Wall she took a second leave to write *Strange Justice: The Selling of Clarence Thomas*, which was nominated for both the National Book Award and the Book Critics' Circle Award for nonfiction in 1994. In early 1995 she became a staff writer for *The New Yorker*. She lives in the Washington area with her husband and baby daughter.

5

JANE MAYER

POLITICS AND PUBLIC AFFAIRS

I'm going to tell you some of the things that are important to me in covering politics, public policy and public affairs. But first I have to say that there's absolutely no doctrine in this field, no right way to do it. Gene Roberts, the editor of the *Philadelphia Inquirer*, has said that while everybody else's reporters zig, he wants his to zag. That's how I've tried to look at a lot of issues and a lot of the beats I've had—to follow my instinct and see what's really interesting, as opposed to the required fare of the day.

So I'm going to give you a few examples, starting with the White House, which is a straitjacket of a beat. "White House reporter" sounds very prestigious, and you certainly are close to a lot of power. But a stenographer would be able to do it just as well. You also have very little choice about what to put in the paper every day. If the President burps, you say the President burped, and that's basically it. So I was frustrated in that beat.

When I started covering Reagan I was 28 and hadn't had a lot of experience covering politics. The day came for my first interview in the Oval Office. It's an annual event for a major newspaper, and it's nervewracking if you're a new reporter; all your editors come in from New York, and you're the reporter asking the questions. But first there's a prep session where they—in my case *The Wall Street Journal*—tell you that the interview should be about tax reform and progressivity of rates and indexing this and that. So in my interview with Reagan I was spewing out statistics like a mainframe computer. But I got through it, and Reagan looked as if it was as much fun for him as it was for me. He clearly wasn't interested in indexing this and that, and at the very end I decided to just throw him an unscripted question—which was risky, because the question would sound idiotic to any normal person. And all my bosses were there. This is by way of saying: always take the risk, just try it. It doesn't matter how foolish you look in this business.

I had heard that Reagan was interested in Armageddon. So I said, "Mr. President, I hear that you're interested in Armageddon, is that right?" And he said, "Well, funny you should ask—I was just talking about it this morning. You know, many people believe that the prophecy may come true soon and that the Soviet Union will be the cause. The clash, if you read the Scriptures, will take place in what is now known as the Middle East. I think there may be something in that." Which is an alarming thought, knowing that this was the man who controlled the world's largest nuclear arsenal.

Now, one of the early warning signs in Washington that you might actually have an interesting story is how the handlers react. Larry Speakes jumped up from the couch and started clearing his throat and lamenting that we had run out of time. So that turned into an interesting story. But to me what was really interesting was this: Odd though Reagan's answer was, it was even odder that when the transcript of the interview came out the next day there was no mention of Armageddon. (Traditionally the White House will put out the transcript of every major news interview so that the rest of the press can write stories from it.) Our entire conversation had been edited down, which was the real story of the Reagan White House; his whole presidency was cropped like a picture to show only the flattering parts.

Writing that Armageddon story became a touchy subject. My paper is very conservative, politically, and generally they don't interfere, but they weren't anxious to do a whole lot with that particular story. So we ran a box. I wrote the main interview, and then I wrote something that ran on the side about his interest in Armageddon, and it was left at that. But other papers picked up the story— which is the point of my telling you about it. It shows why the odd question, the unexpected question, is often the good question. You get unexpected answers, unscripted answers. In this case, the story was a window into Reagan's mind. It showed not only how ignorant he was in some ways but also how superstitious and strangely fatalistic he was about these things. It gives you some insight into why he would have been the person to make the deal with Gorbachev, knowing what he thought he was up against—some sort of nuclear holocaust that was five minutes away, according to the Bible.

In the Reagan years the White House was geared as a public-relations operation. They would build the day around the evening news broadcast. So it was impenetrable. But it was also very time-consuming, because they didn't make it easy. They made you go on trips to Ohio that would take up your whole day, and you weren't near phones where you could call people and find out anything else. It made me think it was a foolish way for news organizations to cover the White House.

I subsequently talked to my paper about it, but they feel that they need someone who's doing a body watch—someone who will be there to file if the President is assassinated, someone to be the stenographer of whatever historical events may happen. So you're a captive of the place. I wasn't under the illusion that I had cracked the joint and knew what was going on. Of all the beats I've covered, the White House was the worst. You just couldn't get your hands around the place. It's a sensory-deprivation tank. Once a week you're allowed out of the pressroom to have your weekly interview with the chief of staff, but otherwise you're sitting there waiting for whatever the next thing is they know you have to cover. Covering Reagan meant having to say you never saw him. Bush was more available and kind of hyper, so you could at least see him. But who knows what was really going on during the Bush years? Maybe we'll find out about Iraqgate and those other events only now that he's out of office.

This business of how the White House cropped pictures—edited Reagan—became the real story of the place for me. I finally decided that I had to leave the White House in order to cover it. My decision to take a leave of absence in 1987 was prompted by the breaking of the Iran-Contra affair. We were sitting one day in the pressroom, where we had scarcely ever seen Reagan; his voice was piped in to us in a disembodied Oz fashion, and we would write our stories from that and pretend we had some real contact, so that everyone in the outside world would think we were important.

But on that particular day a sleazy Lebanese newspaper broke the Iran-Contra story, and Ed Meese, the attorney general, had to tell us, while we were sitting there, what the actual news was that we had missed during all those three years—that a President who had said he was never going to deal with terrorists had in fact been sending them huge amounts of weapons and then diverting the profits to Nicaragua, where he was funding a secret war that he had promised Congress was over. It was astounding to me that we had been sitting there for three years, following photo opportunities and being run ragged like hamsters on a wheel, and meanwhile all these important events were unfolding right in the same building, literally on the other side of the wall.

So I thought: we've been had. This situation requires more close reporting, and if I stay on this beat I'm not going to have the time to do it. So I got a book contract with Houghton Mifflin and took a leave, and got a co-author, Doyle McManus, who knew parts of the story that I didn't know, and we spent the next year writing the book, which was called *Landslide: The Unmaking of the President.* One big advantage was that I already had sources, which is important in covering public affairs. I knew many of the players by then, well enough so that they would return my phone calls. And I found that people who had been reticent when I quoted them for the next day's newspaper got more and more comfortable giving longer interviews for a book, as I kept going back to them. They would talk and see that there was no repercussion and talk some more.

So I was able to get all kinds of stories I never would have been able to get if I had been on a newspaper, including one from several top aides at the White House, who told me they had been very concerned about Reagan becoming despondent and out of it. They said he would sit in the Oval Office watching television a lot during the day, and at one point they actually met and talked about invoking the 25th Amendment, which allows for the involuntary retirement of the President if he can no longer carry out his duties.

That story wasn't easy to pin down. I interviewed one aide several times, and he never did confide in me, but he did mention somebody else, who knew more about it. It was only when I asked that person directly that he came forward and talked about it and even brought his notes from the meeting. If you're going to get into something as dicey as a President possibly being impeached by his own staff, you'd better have something to back it up with. In this case I not only had copies of my informant's notes; I had an agreement that if I showed him how the section would appear in the book and he was happy with it, he would stand up later, when there was publicity, and say it was true. That became a godsend, because when the book came out and the story broke and *Nightline* called, the first thing they did was call him, and he agreed to go on the air and back it up. If he had said, "I don't know what she's talking about," that would probably have been the end of the book, and it wouldn't have been too good for me either.

Q. Who was that man?

His name was Jim Cannon. He had been an aide to Gerald Ford in the Ford White House and had also been an aide in the latter years of the Reagan White House.

Q. Were there any repercussions? Did he have anything to lose?

I was amazed that he would tell me all this. In fact, he wasn't alone; other White House aides corroborated my story. One of them was former chief of staff Howard Baker. Before the book came out I got a letter from him, saying, "Yes, this account seems accurate to me." I don't think those men had anything to gain. But I do think there's an appeal, when someone is writing about public affairs, especially if it's a book, that you're writing history, or at least a rough draft of history. Most people who are involved in politics have some dream of playing a part in history, and you're the person who is compiling it. If you demonstrate that you're sincere and making every effort to be accurate and to go over your drafts with the people involved, they will cooperate for the longer haul. There really wasn't anything in it for Mr. Cannon. Fortunately, I don't think he suffered from it, because by the time the book was published Reagan's reputation was being reexamined, and a lot of people who had been saying "He's not what he seems to be" were looking smart for saying it. It's a question of timing.

But what I'm really talking about are conventions: how to break out of the straitjacket of conventional reporting and look at things a little differently. This approach has yielded many of my best stories But it's also risky. So if you're going to follow your gut, which I think everybody ought to do, you should realize that you're flying solo and should take all precautions. Be sure everything you've got is 100 percent accurate.

Let me tell you about a time when I did not do that and crashed and burned in a spectacular fiasco. In my earliest days as a reporter I was covering City Hall for the *Washington Star*, which was the definitely dead-end number-two paper in town. I was out in the suburbs; my beat was Alexandria, and it was deadly—just covering one late-night zoning meeting after another. I got so that I could write 15 inches of copy in 15 minutes. Those meetings would go until one in the morning, and the biggest challenge was to stay awake. So in my effort to zag instead of zig I thought I could beat out my competition, which was mainly the *Washington Post*, by being more inventive.

One day I was flipping through the city directory, looking for interesting stories that somebody might not have thought of, and I guess I didn't get much further than *A*—to the city arborist. I thought: Great, I'll interview the city arborist. He must be a waste of city funds. Why does the city need an arborist? I called the man, and as we talked he handed me a whopping story. He said he had been taking bribes. It was the last thing I had expected to hear. He told me he had been taking money for planting trees in front of good developments, and the developers would pay him off.

I thought: Wow, great story, front-page play out of this awful town. So I ran with it, and of course they did play it on the front page—municipal corruption. Well, I hadn't thought too much about why this man might be telling me this, or bothered to check it or talk to the developers, or anything like that. So the next day, after this splashy story came out, the city attorney dragged the arborist in to interview him. After a couple of hours they gave him a lie-detector test and found that he had made the whole thing up. So it turned out that there were reasons why I was the sole reporter on the story. His credibility was dead, and mine was pretty close.

There's an important lesson in this, which is that public officials and other people lie. They lie for reasons that are often unimaginable and sometimes irrational. To this day I have no idea why that man was more interested in planting stories than in planting trees. He lost his job over it, and it was clear that I should have checked with quite a few other people before running with the story.

Q. You mean your editors ran with a one-source story?

Yes, they did; it was not a first-rate newspaper. You'd also be surprised how sloppy a lot of editors are. But as a reporter the mistake is yours, not theirs. You go into a job possessing a certain amount of trust until you make a mistake like that, and then they look at you cross-eyed for the next two years.

Since then I've covered a number of people in high office who lie through their teeth, including many in the Reagan White House. You're pretty defenseless with a public official who is lying, because you can't say he's lying unless you can prove he's lying, and you can be so easily misled. You must double-check everything. You can't imagine the things people make up.

One of the the things I've been lucky with is broadly defining any beat I've been given. Beats can be constricting. Some people think that if you cover City Hall you should never talk to anyone outside City Hall. But I urge anybody whose job is to cover a narrow assignment to interview everyone who touches your beat. Interview the caterers who come in with the food, interview the photographers who take the pictures. Talk to relatives. Talk to officials who come in contact with the person you're covering. Those things can lead to wonderful stories, and generally people who are on the periphery are looser with the details than those who are working for the person you're covering. Someone whose writing I especially admire is Maureen Dowd of *The New York Times*. She gets some of her best facts from photographers and other so-called peripheral people.

Going at your beat in a broader sense, you should try to imagine how you can push the limits of interesting news that's related to it. Once, when I was covering television, a beat that can be interpreted very narrowly, I persuaded one editor—this could only happen at a paper like *The Wall Street Journal* that has a decent bankroll—that a great story would be a profile of the best war-zone cameraman in the world. I wanted to write about how it's the cameramen who really have to take the risks and be right there in the action. They also have to be unusual people, who want to go from war to war to war. At that particular time, in 1983, one of the wars was in Beirut. I was sitting in New York covering the networks, and we didn't have a reporter in Beirut, and my editor said, "Sure, go ahead."

I flew to Beirut to write about this cameraman, Alan De Bos, who made a wonderful subject. And while I was there the U.S. Marine barracks was blown up and 241 marines were killed. I was the only reporter on the scene, so I covered the news. The lesson is to be open to sudden and even terrible changes at the last minute. If you're in a place to cover a story, but something else is happening that you can imagine pushing to the limit and doing something interesting with, do it. One piece usually leads to another. While I was in the Beirut hotel filing those stories about the Marine barracks, our Washington bureau chief called and said, "We want you to cover the presidential campaign. Can you move to Washington?"

Not all my suggestions of broadly interpreted beats have been accepted. One winter in Washington it was cold and dreary, and I was supposed to be covering politics. I tried to convince my editor that the Guam primary was a must of a story, much misunderstood. He said, "It smells of suntan lotion." Still, it's always worth a try.

Actually I did get one suntan on the paper's payroll. By then I was covering the White House, and Reagan was doing a staged photo op in Grenada to revisit the triumph of his invasion and celebrate the victory. He was going to give a speech, stand in front of the palm trees, and come home again. So I went a week earlier to do a story about the advance work that goes into a photo opportunity like that. My paper was nice to let me do it, because it meant a week in Grenada in February, but it turned out to be an incredibly interesting story. I was trying to calculate how much everything was costing—huge transport planes were flying in every hour with props and equipment for the press. I got someone to tell me that the visit Reagan was making was going to cost between $3 million and $5 million—just a fly-in and fly-out. It was a great look behind the scenes, which is often worth doing when you're covering politics, especially since so much of it is now geared for television; people never see anything except what they're meant to see. That was another example of zagging.

It was also an example of a story where you don't win friends among the people you're covering. When I returned from Grenada, all the appointments I had with people at the White House were mysteriously canceled. Every single one. The press secretary had evidently put me on what he called his "death list." It was terrible. You can pay a price for this kind of reporting. I couldn't even find out where the President was going to be the next day. My editors would say, "Where's Reagan going to be?" and I would say, "I've got to get back to you on that." And finally I would have to call a friend and ask, because nobody at the White House would tell me anything. What Larry Speakes used to love to say was, "I'm putting you out of business." A reporter friend of mine who suffered that fate had a "going out of business sale" on the front lawn of the White House. He took all the furniture from his little office and stuck it out there with a big sign. If you write stories that are off the beaten track and not what they're looking for, you can expect your life to become difficult.

Q. Going back to Maureen Dowd, whom you mentioned earlier, the piece she wrote in *The New York Times* the day after the 1992 presidential election was an amazing article. It was a devastating indictment of George Bush—how his flaws of character had brought about his defeat—and it was really more of an editorial than a news story. Would newspapers have been allowed to run that kind of writing five years ago?

I think Maureen has expanded the barriers in covering politics, in ways that earlier reporters weren't able to, and part of it is because she writes so well. She's extremely careful—she doesn't make mistakes, so they trust her. And the *Times* is in a period when it's trying to attract writers who have a highly personal point of view; it used to be more like the Associated Press. In Maureen's case it works really well. I agree that it was a devastating piece. But don't forget that she had done more than most reporters to humanize George Bush. She was the one who originally wrote about how he liked pork rinds and country music. She asked questions that other reporters didn't ask, to try to get a sense of what kind of person he was.

Q. I guess my question is: Has objectivity, the sacred goal we were all reared on, been redefined in an unspoken way?

I think so, largely because of CNN and C-SPAN television. You've got CNN covering the camera's-eye view of events, and on C-SPAN viewers can see public policy hearings, so the conventional press is trying to figure out a role for itself. That may be why you see the *Times* moving in that direction.

Another unexpected story of mine resulted from a fairly conventional assignment to cover a bit of the Persian Gulf war. I was sent to Cairo, which was not the scene of the main action but a good place to monitor the Arab political world and write stories about diplomatic developments in the Arab countries. It didn't sound as if it was going to be fascinating, but I thought it was worth a try, and I had never been to Cairo.

On the night the United States began bombing Baghdad I went down to the lobby to look for some Kuwaitis—I was in a luxury hotel, where many Kuwaitis were living. None of them were to be found. So I asked the bellman if he had seen any Kuwaitis. He was an Egyptian, and most of the Egyptians in Cairo are very poor, and he said with a sneer, "Oh, yes, they're out slugging out the war in the discothèque." I went up to the hotel's discothèque to see what was going on, and sure enough, the Kuwaitis were dancing. That was a case where someone's offhand remark sparks a story, which was: Why is it that American soldiers are fighting in Kuwait and flying bombing missions to Baghdad when draft-age Kuwaiti men are dancing over here in a discothèque?

So I asked some of them about it, and they were shamelessly arrogant, saying the kinds of things an editor would die to print—about how they were rich enough to buy others to do their soldiering for them. It was a devastating story, and it ran on the front page of *The Wall Street Journal* and won a prize for the best story of the Gulf war. This isn't to say that I'm a genius and the people who were covering the Gulf war from the press pool in Kuwait, where they never got to see anything, were morons. It's more a matter of just keeping your ears open. My beat was not the glamour beat, but this argues for the uses of adversity. Again, it's a matter of going with your gut when something looks interesting. It wasn't what I was sent to Cairo to do, but it became a fine story that was right in front of me.

Another unheroic aspect of that Cairo story, but one that's instructive, is that I didn't know that the United States had started bombing Baghdad. It was about one o'clock in the morning, Cairo time, and I had gone to sleep, and none of my editors had thought to call and tell me about the bombing. I wouldn't have known it was going on except that I got a warning call from another American reporter in Cairo, which is not what anyone would expect when you're all competitors. But I had been in Cairo long enough to hang out with other reporters and develop some fellowship. This wouldn't be pertinent if you were doing what's called enterprise reporting, or if you had found a great story on your own. But with the bombing, if you had been watching CNN you would have known about it; it was a world fact. I tell you this by way of saying that often, when you're writing about a subject that other people are also covering, life is less perilous and much more fun if you develop a bit of collegiality.

I've certainly worked with people who didn't feel that way. Once when I was on the *Washington Star*, I was covering a trial when I got sick to my stomach. I remember telling my competitor, the guy from the *Washington Post*, "I've got to go throw up in the bathroom. Could you cover for me?" and he said "No." But I've had a lot of help over the years and have been able to give other people help on things that really are matters of luck, not talent. It has led to many good friendships.

In all those big stories, the news that you're sent to cover already exists. But I've also written many stories on policy issues, which by their nature are abstract and hard to make interesting, especially if you're writing about a dry policy debate. What works best, I think, is to try to particularize the story and find a living illustration. Most government policies involve real people in one way or another, and if you can find some of the people who are affected—or even find an interesting bureaucrat—getting them to explain the story brings it home to people.

Once I was covering the war on drugs and the debate about how to handle crack: what social services the government should pay for and what it could afford to pay for. I wanted to find some interesting stories that would illustrate the issue, not just tear-jerking stories. So I started calling police departments around the country in places where I knew there was a lot of crack, to ask how crack had affected their area. Finally I settled on a story—a very extreme story—in Opalocka, Florida, outside Miami, about a woman named Wanda McNeil. She was a crack addict so desperate for money that she sold her baby for three dollars. The police blotter said: "June 4, a man was quoted by the police as saying he 'bought a baby for $3 from a woman who stated she have a baby and will kill it if she don't get three dollars.'"

Not knowing what I was going to find, I flew to Miami and rented a car and drove to Opalocka. First I went to the police, because they would be my guides; it's a dangerous story, and you want to know what you should and shouldn't do. I felt that what was absolutely essential was to be able to name the woman and all the people involved—their whole names, not something like "Shirley B." I wanted the veracity that can come only from real people, and to interview them and have them all on the record, talking.

Well, I found the mother, and the things she told me were shocking to readers of *The Wall Street Journal*. She said that when the baby was born she had been doing so many drugs that "when they told me the baby had ten fingers and ten toes I nearly fainted." She didn't know who the father was. She talked about life on the street, and she gave a very descriptive account of what was so great about crack, how it made her feel: "You can't do your homework, you can't go to work, you can't clean the yard, you can't do anything but think about getting more. I like the hit that goes right to my brain—makes your eyes pop and your toes wiggle. You can't get enough of it. After a while your heart starts pounding. It makes you relax and enjoy life, and that's what life's about, enjoying it."

This is to say that the more specific you can be in describing a problem—finding a real person to talk about it in her own voice—the more powerful it's going to be in driving it home to people. I didn't only want to talk to that woman; I wanted to get a sense of where she came from. So I went to Atlanta and interviewed her mother and found out what kind of family she belonged to. She was one of 17 children. Then I interviewed Johnny Wind, known as "Geech," who bought the baby, about why he had bought it. He was a derelict. He turned out not to be a bad guy at all; he was someone who thought the mother was going to kill the baby, so he gave her the money. It wasn't exactly that he wanted the baby. He told me, "I've got eight children myself that I can't take care of as it is. What do I want with buying one more?"

But beyond this tragic, terrible story of how drugs destroy people's families, I thought it was important to raise the issue of what was going to happen with the legal system and the social services. The woman had been in and out of various treatment centers, and there was a question of whether she should keep custody of the kid. So I talked to all the judges and social service agency people who were dealing with this case and had dealt with similar cases, and the outcome surprised me, because they decided to let the mother keep the baby. "What are we going to do with all these kids?" they said. "We can't take them all."

Q. Did your story leave the reader with one point, or one way of thinking about it?

I'm not sure. I thought the mother seemed like a lost cause. But the alternatives were problematical too. She had had another kid, who also had fallen into a bad situation and was in an institution that was costing taxpayers $97,000 a year. I left it as a debate, because to me it's a policy debate—a social issue. What do you do with such tragic people? What do you do with the kids, and what can the courts and agencies handle?

Actually the mother was very articulate on why she wanted to keep the baby. She was angry that they could conceivably take it away—this was after the baby had been given back to her. She said "White women want to take other people's kids because they think they can rear them better. White women are scared to have their own babies because they're thinking more about their shapes and their careers." She knew what she wanted.

Q. What's the paragraph like in which you somewhat state your own opinion?

My opinion is sort of infused in the story, because you can see that the mother is such a danger to her own child. Near the end I quote a worker in one of the social agencies saying this about parental rights: "The judges say give the mother a chance, but I say you're not giving the child a chance. It would be great if we had programs to save the mothers and the children, but as it is, I think we have to perform triage. Why wait until there's more neglect and more abuse when the child is a couple of years older? When do you say enough is enough?" Partly by positioning that quote near the end, where I was summarizing, I left that idea with the reader. But you never can tell.

Q. How did you talk the woman into talking with you?

It wasn't anything too fancy. It was a matter of her standing me up on a number of occasions and my just continuing to call her and arranging to meet her in places that were hard to find. It took a long time before she showed up, and when we

finally did do the interview we were sitting on the curb of a
7-Eleven. Altogether, I was there for a week, trying to get the
interview and to get a sense of the place. It was much more
dangerous than any of the wars I've covered.

Q. Why would she consent to talk with you?

I would say, "Your story is important and I'm interested in
what happened. The police say this is what happened, and is
that what happened?" You have to be honest. You can't say,
"I'm going to put you on Oprah tomorrow," or something
like that. There are increasing numbers of people you interview who will say, "What's in it for me?" And often there's
nothing in it for them. You can't promise them anything.

   Her mother was also very hard to get to. She was bedrid-
den, and she only talked to me for a few minutes. I had to go
to a housing project and wait outside until I could talk one of
the kids into letting me in. She wouldn't talk to me on the
phone. And she was really sad—she was crying when I did
finally get in. You feel terrible. I asked two questions and had
to leave. I wanted to find out what had happened to her 17
children; my idea was to do a history of the family—a *Roots*
kind of story that would explain how a family gets into such
an advanced state of decay. What had been their history and
their experience? What had they told each other from one
generation to the next? But because the mother wouldn't
cooperate I couldn't do it.

   I did one other drug story, which I thought worked out
well. Again, it was an effort to try to explain the larger phenomenon of the spread of crack. First I went to the Drug
Enforcement Administration and looked at their reports
about where the drug was reaching the country. This was
several years ago, when the drug was brand-new. I found a
small town called Seaford, Delaware, which was an Ozzie-
and-Harriet kind of town, mostly white and middle class. I
hadn't really been conscious of it, but I'm sure that in the

back of my mind was: "My readers think this is something that just happens in the ghetto and they don't care. But I can make them care if I write about a problem in a way that says, 'It could happen here, it could be you, it could be your kids.'" One journalistic problem is that a lot of readers overlook stories that happen to people very different from themselves.

What interested me was a DEA report that said migrant workers brought in the crops in Seaford. They included a lot of Haitians who had moved to Florida and brought crack with them up the Eastern corridor. I wanted to write about this town in a way that would be like explaining what would happen if you put poison in the water system. What happens to a town when something lethal and dangerous like that hits? It was a small enough place so that you could do an anatomy, or an autopsy, of the town. I wrote about how a series of crimes had hit this little town in a way that was different from any other kind of crime they had ever had. Many were vicious murders by people who were high on crack. I read about those murders, and visited the emergency room and the neonatal ward and the schools, and tried to follow how the drug had infiltrated the community. The community itself was up in arms, so there were many very concerned civic-minded people who were trying to do something about it. The story worked well, I think, in a way that just writing up the DEA report wouldn't have worked: "Crack has now reached 450 small towns in the Northeast." The job is to take the statistic and make it real.

Q. How does what you're doing differ from being just a feature writer? Are you a political reporter by definition, by assignment?

My beat is public affairs and public policy, and most of the stories I write get back to a debate over public policy. What should you do? What should be done? What should the DEA do? Does the DEA have enough people to control this kind of flow of drugs? How about the Haitians? And immigration policy? What interests me are fights over issues and the whole process of how this country decides what's the right thing to do.

I'm now writing a book on the Anita Hill–Clarence Thomas case. It's by far the hardest thing I've ever done, and certainly the least fun. It's just been one wall after the next that I've had to batter down, with my head. The book grew out of the same sense I had covering the White House and having the Iran-Contra affair presented to us and thinking: Hey, we missed the story—there was a story here.

I had watched the hearings like everybody else and knew that one of those two people was lying. It was a national mystery. There had to be a way to find out where the truth was, and either way it was a terrible thing. If it turned out that she was lying, someone should clear Clarence Thomas's name. If he was lying, it was one of the most cynical political spectacles in a long time, which tarnished Congress and the Supreme Court in a way they hadn't been tarnished before.

I thought: This is what I'm trained to do. There's got to be a way to do it. So I got another leave of absence and another contract from Houghton Mifflin, and I got the transcripts of the hearings, and I set out to interview every single person over again, and to go to Oklahoma to find out who Anita Hill really was, and to go to Pinpoint, Georgia, and other places to try to interview the far-flung Thomas family and follow their tracks over the years and see if I could figure out what the truth was.

The Washington end of the story is possible for me to do. The other part is harder. Writing about gender issues—the politics of being in the women's movement—is something I can write about from the gut because I understand it; it comes from my experience. On the other hand, writing about race in this case is incredibly complicated. It had never occurred to me that there would be so many people I had to interview, who, even if they were sympathetic to one side or the other, absolutely refused to talk about it because they think the whole thing was such a blemish and an embarrassment. They don't want to see anything more written on it. I've had to spend a tremendous amount of time begging people for interviews, writing letters, pleading with them, trying to explain that I'm fair and credible. I'm trying to jump over the chasm of race in this country, which is far wider than I had ever realized when I was reporting on it. But I think we'll have a book. I say "we" because I have a coauthor again. Book writing is a solitary profession, and I enjoy having somebody to work with.

Q. How do you collaborate on a project like this?

On the last book it was easy. I had covered the White House, and Doyle McManus had covered foreign affairs. Before the Iran-Contra affair he had been to Nicaragua and all over the Middle East; he knew the State Department people and the whole broad side of the story. I knew the White House, so it was easy to divide who had what areas of expertise. We then did an outline and divided up chapters and gave each other notes on the parts we knew about in each other's chapters. Then we wrote drafts of the chapters and handed them back and forth and corrected them and turned them into a book. He's a delightful person and an incredibly good reporter, so it worked out well.

On the present book I'm working with Jill Abramson, who was also on *The Wall Street Journal*. She's a much better investigative reporter than I am. I'm probably a better writer, but she's an incredible digger. We began by making lists of people we had to interview, and then we divided them, mostly on the basis of people we've known before. Inside the White House there are some people I know and some people she knows. On the Hill, I've got the Democrats and she's got the Republicans. We do most of our interviews separately. Then we hand each other the transcripts and get together every few days to talk about it. I'm encouraged because we've found some really interesting things that haven't been revealed before. But both of us have found it incredibly hard.

Q. Will you reach a verdict in the book?

Only if the facts support one.

POSTSCRIPT

WILLIAM ZINSSER • "Has objectivity, the sacred goal we were all reared on, been redefined in an unspoken way?" That question, asked of Jane Mayer in connection with Maureen Dowd's morning-after election piece in *The New York Times*, bobbed up in several sessions of our class, a troubling presence. John Tierney first mentioned it, describing his coverage of the 1992 New Hampshire Presidential primaries. When he wrote that Paul Tsongas was a "messianic pedant" the *Times* didn't reassign him to some less seductive beat like the Sanitation Department, as would have happened in my newspaper days. It labeled his articles "Campaign Watch" to serve notice that they were in the nature of a column, not a news story. Explaining that *Times* reporters are now urged to write distinctively, Tierney said, "My editors encouraged me to write with as much voice and opinion as I wanted." Melinda Beck of *Newsweek*, in Chapter 8, recalls being surprised by her magazine's coverage of that same election, which "consisted of four dueling columnists offering their own take on the political news. In the old days such pieces would have been four sidebars around the main story. Now they *are* the main story."

I vividly remember Maureen Dowd's election postmortem, which ran on the front page of the *Times*. Analyzing the causes of George Bush's defeat, it noted that as early as 1991, 75 percent of Americans felt that the country was "on the wrong track," and it went on to say:

Mr. Bush did not care. From the beginning of his administration it was clear that he had no ideas or programs he wanted to enact, that his greatest pleasure came from simply being President. After his first hundred days in office it was clear that he was practicing the politics of minimalism. . . . Unlike Mr. Reagan, Mr. Bush had no fixed principles to fall back on, because his ideology was friendship. So he was only as good or as bad as the advisers he relied on, and many of his advisers were remarkably inept and unpopular. . . . [He] had no feel for capturing and projecting the fears, angers and delights of the American public. Words meant little to him. . . . When Mr. Bush broke the "Read My Lips" pledge about taxes and made the joke "Read My Hips," he truly believed that Americans did not expect politicians to keep such pledges.

As a voter I found the piece gratifying; it summed up many of my deepest reasons for having wanted the President out. But as a journalist I felt slightly uneasy: Dowd had been allowed to present as certitudes a set of personal opinions and inferences. Were they correct? Almost surely they were; Mr. Bush had been her beat, and she knew him better than most reporters. Were they provable? No. They were not quite facts. They were artifacts of the new terrain that reporters are staking out, pushed into conjecture by competition from CNN and C-SPAN television.

"I think Maureen has expanded the barriers in covering politics in ways that earlier reporters weren't able to," Jane Mayer said, "and part of it is because she writes so well." An interesting point. Good writing is always an occasion for gratitude in the turbid gray mass of the daily paper; I keep a lookout for reporters who will brighten my day with a style that sets them apart from reporters who are merely competent. I still remember discovering a *Times* cub sports reporter named Gay Talese, writing a hilarious piece about a boxer in Cut 'n' Shoot, Texas. The kid went on to become a coinventor of the New Journalism. John Tierney told our class that he went to Yale intending to major in mathematics. He said I met him at a freshman reception and encouraged him to sign up for my writing workshop. I must have detected a spark that I thought would be lost in the world of sines and cosines. I didn't know I was launching him on the road to calling Paul

Tsongas a messianic pedant.

But should good writers be able to get away with more than dull writers? Is elegance a license to editorialize? The answer, I suppose, is that finally there's no holding a really good writer down. The most influential reporter in American journalism, H. L. Mencken, achieved that legendary status by combining a pyrotechnical style with a view of human nature that took no prisoners. Compare what Maureen Dowd wrote about George Bush in 1992 to what Mencken wrote in 1933, in the Baltimore *Evening Sun*, about an earlier President, Calvin Coolidge, who had just died:

> The editorial writers who had the job of concocting mortuary tributes to the late Calvin Coolidge, LL.D., made heavy weather of it, and no wonder. Ordinarily, an American public man dies by inches, and there is thus plenty of time to think up beautiful nonsense about him. More often than not, indeed, he threatens to die three or four times before he actually does so, and each threat gives the elegists a chance to mellow their effusions. But Dr. Coolidge slipped out of life almost as quietly and as unexpectedly as he had originally slipped into public notice, and in consequence the brethren were caught napping and had to do their poetical embalming under desperate pressure. The common legend is that such pressure inflames and inspires a true journalist, and maketh him to sweat masterpieces, but it is not so in fact. Like any other literary man, he functions best when he is at leisure, and can turn from his tablets now and then to run down a quotation, to eat a plate of ham and eggs, or to look out of the window.
>
> The general burden of the Coolidge memoirs was that the right hon. gentleman was a typical American, and some hinted that he was the most typical since Lincoln. As the English say, I find myself quite unable to associate myself with that thesis. He was, in truth, almost as unlike the average of his countrymen as if he had been born green. The Americano is an expansive fellow, a back-slapper, full of amiability; Coolidge was reserved and even muriatic.

The Americano has a stupendous capacity for believing, and especially for believing in what is palpably not true; Coolidge was, in his fundamental metaphysics, an agnostic. The Americano dreams vast dreams, and is hag-ridden by a demon; Coolidge was not mount but rider, and his steed was a mechanical horse. The Americano, in his normal incarnation, challenges fate at every step and his whole life is a struggle; Coolidge took things as they came. . . .

No other President ever slipped into the White House so easily, and none other ever had a softer time of it while there. When, at Rapid City, S.D., on August 2, 1927, he loosed the occult words, "I do not choose to run in 1928," was it prescience or only luck? For one, I am inclined to put it down to luck. Surely there was no prescience in his utterances and maneuvers otherwise. He showed not the slightest sign that he had smelt black clouds ahead; on the contrary, he talked and lived only sunshine. There was a volcano boiling under him, but he did not know it, and was not singed. When it burst forth at last, it was Hoover who got its blast, and was fried, boiled, roasted and fricasseed. How Dr. Coolidge must have chuckled in his retirement, for he was not without humor of a sad, necrotic kind. He knew Hoover well, and could fathom the full depths of the joke.

In what manner he would have performed himself if the holy angels had shoved the Depression forward a couple of years—this we can only guess, and one man's hazard is as good as another's. My own is that he would have responded to bad times precisely as he responded to good ones—that is, by pulling down the blinds, stretching his legs upon his desk, and snoozing away the lazy afternoons. Here, indeed, was his one peculiar *Fach*, his one really notable talent. He slept more than any other President, whether by day or by night. Nero fiddled, but Coolidge only snored. When the crash came at last and Hoover began to smoke and bubble, good Cal was safe in Northampton, and still in the hay.

MARK SINGER has been a staff writer on *The New Yorker* since 1974, writing hundreds of "Talk of the Town" pieces as well as profiles, reporter-at-large pieces and occasional fiction. His first book, *Funny Money*, an account of the collapse of the Penn Square Bank in Oklahoma City, was published in 1985 by Alfred A. Knopf and was on *The New York Times* best-seller list. His second book, *Mr. Personality*, a collection of *New Yorker* profiles and pieces, was published in 1989. His book about Brett Kimberlin, the subject of his 1992 *New Yorker* article that was a finalist for a National Magazine Award in reporting, will be published by Knopf in early 1996.

He lives in Pelham, New York, with his three sons.

6

MARK SINGER

WRITING ABOUT PEOPLE

I went to work at *The New Yorker* in 1974, writing "Talk of the Town" pieces, and what recurred in all those pieces was dialogue. I was learning how to listen to people and trying to capture on the page how they spoke. I actually took a shorthand course because I thought it was important to get dialogue as accurately as possible.

At the same time I was learning another skill, which was reporting: How do you gather the details? If you walk into a room you have to describe what's going on in that room. If you talk to a person, at some point you have to render a portrait of that person. What does the person look like? What are his or her physical characteristics and tics? How does he or she dress? But you don't dump all those details in the reader's lap at once. The idea is to build a scene, and you build it with these bits of exposition and narration, along with dialogue.

What has always driven me as a writer is that I'm curious

about people. I just want to know. I get to learn about the world through the experiences of the people I write about. I've written articles about many different fields, all over the country, but always at the core of those articles is an interesting person.

In the early years of my career, New York was the greatest laboratory imaginable. I was 24 years old and I had grown up in Tulsa, Oklahoma. So it was all new to me. Many people have the impression that "Talk of the Town" stories are written by monocled sophisticates who look like Eustace Tilley. But remarkably often those pieces have been written by Midwesterners, absolute out-of-towners. When I was a boy in Tulsa we had an extended family living in Oklahoma City, which was 100 miles away, and we visited one another regularly. Four carfuls of people would arrive on a Sunday afternoon, and what I would notice was that Cousin Bessie wasn't there; I was the one who somehow kept track of who was who. These people were my universe. To this day, when I go back, I'll be talking with my father about some fairly obscure subject and I'll have a store of memories of these people—who was whose cousin, what business they were in. Why that is I don't know. I often wish I could get rid of all this stuff.

That curiosity became one of my main qualifications for writing profiles as an adult. I immerse myself in my subject. When I'm writing a profile I really don't want to be working on anything else, because I want to enter into that person's world, so that I become familiar not only with my subject's own experiences but with who his friends are and with the anecdotes he tells me that lead me to other anecdotes and other friends. I recently finished writing a profile of the magician Ricky Jay, who is, among other things, a sleight-of-hand artist, a rare-book dealer, and an expert on frauds and con games. He's an intensely private person, first about the techniques of magic; he doesn't want them revealed. He had an unhappy childhood, and as I began to interview him he was very concerned about his privacy being violated. But I think I was just so persistent that eventually he had me calling up people he knew to ask them questions. So finally I was able to construct a schematic model of his universe. It took months, but the result was that his life and his work and his network of friendships were just sitting there somewhere behind my frontal lobes for as long as I needed to write the piece. Now it will all wash away.

But there are hazards in immersing yourself too long in a profile. You not only lose money; you lose the initial freshness and the interest that attracted you to it in the first place, because it's inevitable—at least for me it's inevitable—that at a certain point you and the subject get very tired of each other. You become part of the scenery, and that's good; you want to become invisible, because that's where the real texture, the real details, emerge. There's no longer a formal distance between you and the subject. In fact, I've often had to protect my subjects from themselves, because we've become so familiar that they reveal parts of their lives I don't think are absolutely necessary. I've written profiles in which the period between the initial encounter and publication is as long as two years. You can't force this rich material to happen; it requires the forbearance of the subject. That has to be agreed to ahead of time. I know I'd be annoyed if someone said, "I want to interview you," and I said, "How much time?" and he said, "A couple of hours," and it ended up taking a couple of months. I tell people up front that this is going to go on for quite a while.

During this process of research and interviewing I make an effort to create a narrative as I go along. If I've witnessed a certain scene I bring my shorthand notes back to my word processor and try to reconstruct the scene that day. If I'm traveling I carry a laptop. It's a very clumsy kind of writing, not even a first draft. But bits of it will emerge in the final article. It gives me a sense of security when I write the article if I have something concrete to go from.

What I hope will begin to emerge is some kind of narrative logic. I find that inside each piece there is a chronological spine. You build a narrative. It doesn't begin at the beginning of the subject's life and end at the present, but somewhere you discover a linear progression whereby you tell this person's biography. It can vary greatly in its shape. For instance, I've interviewed people who wanted to talk about themselves only in the present, not in the past, so the narrative gets greatly reduced. But structurally there's always a chronological thread that gives the story a logic.

Writing about people, you enter into the lives of your subjects in ways that differ from one story to another. One of my profiles was about the five Brennan brothers, who were apartment superintendents in New York. I was in their homes; I was in their offices; I attended family gatherings over a long period of time. We became social friends; when their mother had an eightieth birthday party I was there; when they had christenings I was there; on St. Patrick's Day I was there. For a story about the Chinos, a family of Japanese-American farmers near San Diego, I spent weeks with them over a long stretch of time, for a few hours a day. I had meals with them and talked with them until eventually I was taken for granted. This will sound peculiar, but I used to feel funny about the Chinos' daily invitation to join them for lunch. I thought: Why do they have to put up with me? Well, the Chinos have a farm lunch every day; one more mouth at the table means nothing, and it also makes them feel good. But it took me a while to just say, "This is the way they live. Anybody who shows up here gets absorbed into this group, and I should just take my seat at the table and not make it seem like a big deal, because it's not a big deal. It's just the way they live."

If I've lost my early fear of being intrusive, it's because I've never written about anyone who finally didn't want to be written about. The initial approach requires overcoming a certain shyness on the part of the subject, but that's easy. I now accept the fact that this is what I do as a reporter.

I'm always trying to become a better listener. Listening is the most important skill in all this. You can't get in the way of the story and still get the story. That was the great fallacy of the

New Journalism, though there were a lot of wonderful things about it. I learned so much by reading Tom Wolfe; his eye for specific details—the source of many exquisite metaphors—was extraordinary. But listening is the key ingredient—just going with the flow, going where your subject has to go, making no demands other than the right to tag along as an observer, not trying to force an event to happen. Sometimes you ask your subject ahead of time, "I notice that you go every Wednesday to such and such. Could I accompany you there?"—knowing it would be a place where you can see him in character and knowing that you're not manufacturing the event. The greatest danger—where the New Journalism often went wrong—is for the writer to become the focal point of the piece.

I've always thought that you can't write well about a subject you're not interested in. What sustains me when I'm writing about people is my curiosity about what it is they do that makes them a good subject. It's also important for me to fundamentally admire something about the person I'm writing about. I wrote one profile, about an art dealer named Graham Arader, who to this day I think is a terrifically interesting guy though in certain respects a destructive person. The piece I wrote reflected that, and he wasn't happy about it. But in no way do I find him uninteresting. He's a fascinating character.

Luckily, my first *New Yorker* profile was about somebody I not only thought was interesting and liked, but truly loved—my great-uncle, Goodman Ace. He was the radio and television comedy writer whose radio show, *Easy Aces*, was full of malaprops delivered by his wife, Jane.

On that story I did something I haven't done since, which was to use a tape recorder, because with Ace it was important to get the words down exactly as he said them. That's a good rationale for taping an interview; otherwise I prefer to take notes. The piece was in many ways about language, because what Goodman Ace was about was the way language plays tricks on the ear.

The most challenging and gratifying thing about doing a profile of "Goody" was writing about a person who was funny: telling readers in the lead, "This man is funny," and then persuading them by offering enough examples, which is a matter of reporting. But there was also a secondary thing going on, which was that I was being slightly funny myself—presenting Ace in a way that was inherently amusing:

Sharing Goodman Ace's company as he ambles through his seventy-ninth year of life, I often get the feeling that I'm watching a lucky and gifted veteran lion tamer work before a largely empty house. Risks ensue and minor mishaps sometimes threaten, but instinct prevails above all. Ace's primary instinct is to be funny, and he almost always is. He says funny things when he talks with his friends, when he rides in a taxi, when he orders lunch at the Friars Club, when he plays pinochle, when he buys cigars, when he goes to the doctor, and even, if his word is to be trusted, when he is all alone. . . .

Gradually a more precise image of the man emerges: the human domino. This is a sterling Aceism that was coined sometime during the thirties or forties, when he wrote, directed, produced, and starred in, along with Jane, "Easy Aces," a seminal radio situation comedy. Many incidents in his life, as Ace recounts them, resemble sitcom. His jokes always have proper contexts. A fair example is his French-restaurant routine, which I have seen him execute several times, although never with any great success. At a certain moment in a French restaurant, Ace motions to a waiter and calls, "Uh, *gendarme*, *gendarme*!" In an ideal world, the waiter will come to the table and politely explain, "Excuse me, monsieur, but I believe you mean to say '*garçon*.' '*Gendarme*' is the French word for policeman." Ace, who lives in this ideal world, will then stare absently at the waiter for a moment and say, "Just the man I want. There seems to be some hold-up in the kitchen." In the real world, unfortunately, few waiters listen closely enough to be able to tell that he has said *gendarme* when he really means *garçon*—thus the empty-house effect.

Not long ago a young woman who had just seen and heard Ace in action for the first time told him, by way of a compliment, that he was the only person she had ever met who "makes up his own jokes." According to his prescription, a worthy joke should be "elegantly phrased and elegantly delivered." Across the years, Ace has written countless jokes, gags, and good stories, which he and other people have brought to life on radio and television, but the best sort of Goodman Ace stories are delivered in person. Ace needs only a chair, a cigar, and, because he is inclined toward both shyness and garrulousness, a slight nudge. He goes to work like a slow-moving roller coaster. The cigar acts as a metronomic device, measuring phrases, coaxing his audience, often sending a loose flutter of ashes tumbling down his shirtfront. In a way, the ashes belong to the delivery. They make the listener suspect that Ace doesn't know where he is going with a story, but he always does. Eventually, one comes to suspect that the ashes fall on cue. Because he chews a cigar as much as he smokes it, moist shreds of tobacco occasionally fall with the ashes, staining his neckties—lovely silk neckties from Sulka and Alexander Shields. "Two experts told me that I absolutely have to give up cigars and ketchup," Ace said recently. "My doctor and my dry cleaner."

What I always try to do, whether I'm writing about murder or show business or street musicians, is to make my subjects come alive for the reader by rendering a colorful portrait of them. I listen carefully to what they say. I'm listening for something that sounds true. There's almost always some human comedy when you're presenting someone in his or her truest light.

"The best malaprops," Ace says, "are those that make a point, such as 'Living in squander'. . . 'Familiarity breeds attempt'. . . 'We're all cremated equal'. . . 'The food in that restaurant was abdominal'. . . 'In all my bored days'. . . 'Every picture I see of Abraham Lincoln makes him look so thin and emancipated.'"

Eventually, "Easy Aces" left its mark on common parlance, and the malaprop that proves a point invariably seems more appropriate than the original phrase. Often janeaceisms—which are, in the first place, goodman-aceisms—creep into Ace's own conversation. Rather than take for granite that Ace talks straight, a listener must be on guard for an occasional entre nous and me. The careful conversationalist might try to mix it up with him in a baffle of wits. In quest of this pinochle of success I have often wrecked my brain for a clowning achievement, but Ace's chickens always come home to roast. It's high noon some-one beat him at his own game, but I have never done it; cross my eyes and hope to die, he always wins thumbs down.

In this kind of writing you're starting with people who are interesting, so they're bound to tell you things that are interesting, or colorful, or amusing. You learn to listen for those things. It might be one of the Brennan brothers, in my profile of those building superintendents, describing his system of having the guys who work for him put their names on their mops and line them up every night so he can tell who is doing a good job and who isn't:

"With the name tapes I can feel the mops, see if they're still wet," George said. "With the padlocks, no one can say he didn't do his work because someone stole his mop or his broom. Each man gets one key to his padlock and I hold one key. You lose your key, you go home with-out pay. Nobody's lost one yet. Check out the mops. You can see who's a pig. You can see who's halfway clean. If it looks rusty, it means they let the mop lie too long in the pail. You can tell by looking which ones I'm concerned about. This cuts out all the nonsense."

A guy talking about the mechanics of running an Upper East Side high-rise—that, to me, can be high comedy.

So was a piece called "Court Buff," a profile of a Brooklyn man named Benjamin Shine who spends his days watching homicide trials—really gruesome stuff. How he makes up his mind about which case he's going to attend—which he often does over lunch in the courthouse cafeteria—is, to him, a fairly straightforward logistical matter. But his description is a litany of the most horrible details you can imagine having to listen to. So he can be talking about a grisly murder while munching a tuna-fish sandwich and meanwhile deciding how he's going to spend the afternoon, and you have something that's funny. I have to do very little work. I'm not nudging the reader; I'm just witnessing the scene and writing it down, because the reader can discern the humor of it himself, without any help. He gets a lot more gratification out of something that comes as a surprise.

You don't want to be in the reader's face at all. *The New Yorker* recently ran a profile of a composer, and what annoyed me was my sense that the writer was less interested in the composer than in his own opinions of him. That's O.K. if you're a critic—your opinions matter a lot. But if you're doing something that's reportorial and narrative, your opinions aren't supposed to take precedence over the subject. It's finally a matter of control. That takes years and years to acquire, and I'm still learning.

I think of each of these pieces as putting together a puzzle. The irony is that I'm lousy at puzzles. But this kind of writing is like an elaborate piece of furniture that requires some fine joinery, and you get out your chisel and you carve the dovetails so that the pieces all fit together. To me that's the great challenge. I love that—figuring out how a thing coheres. When I write a piece I take all these notes. If it's a 15,000-word article I've probably got 60,000 words of notes, so there's a lot of winnowing to be done. I organize the material thematically. I identify the key themes I've discovered while doing the reporting. Then I have to write a lead—and as we all know, nothing happens until you have the lead. Once I have the lead, the real fun begins.

Every piece presents a new problem. Each puzzle has something unique about it. Often I'll go back and read earlier things I've written to try (a) to remind myself that I solved the problem once and therefore it can be solved, and (b) to get some technical pointers. When I first started out I was reading other writers—Calvin Trillin, maybe, or John McPhee, or A. J. Liebling—to see how they solved these puzzles. Often I read fiction. I find that if I read Philip Roth on just about anything I'm listening to an authorial voice so clear that it helps. It's not that I mimic Roth; it's that I'm able to get in touch with my own true voice. But for those technical, almost architectural problems I read nonfiction reporting.

Unfortunately, if you're a young writer, the sad truth is that experience helps—it's a catch-22. You don't have to write *War and Peace* your first day on the job. I wrote hundreds of unsigned "Talk of the Town" pieces, so I didn't have to be haunted by my byline on the ones that fell a little short. I also wrote a number of good pieces that I didn't get the glory for, so there was a trade-off. But I loved the anonymity, and I think that's something to bear in mind. A byline is not necessarily what you want at certain points in your career. The exercise of writing is what matters, and the ego should be gratified by that.

I'm not suggesting that I'm without ego—I want recognition at the right time for what I write. But I was spared a lot of embarrassment by writing unsigned pieces. Before my senior year at college I was hired for the summer by my hometown newspaper, the *Tulsa Tribune*. I had never written for a paper. My first day on the job I had to write about the closing of a town dump. There had been a big storm, and one of the dumps was filled with downed tree branches, so people had to take their storm debris to another dump. I wrote about seven paragraphs, which an editor boiled down to one paragraph, and it ran as a box, with a little border around it, because it was an important public notice, saying that if you had stuff to send to the dump, don't send it to the west side of town, take it to the east side of town.

I took the newspaper home and showed it to my father, and his reaction was that he realized for the first time that everything he read in print had actually been written by someone. I said, "There's no roomful of monkeys with typewriters; there are no mechanical linotype machines doing that. Actually a human mind had to do that." My father is a sophisticated and intelligent man, but this was a revelation to him, and his reaction was a revelation to me—that people had this notion. It made me think that some-body needs to write about the dump closing, and I don't need a byline for the dump closing. I just need to get the information out.

Over the years I've gravitated toward more serious sub-jects, almost by accident, although one could say there are no accidents in these things. I went home to Oklahoma for a family visit in the summer of 1982, when my son Jeb was not quite a year old. All my brothers and sisters were there, and on that trip my firstborn child took his first steps. I had writ-ten about Oklahoma previously; obviously we write about what we know about, and that was a place I knew well and continue to know well. My visit happened to coincide with the failure of a little bank in Oklahoma City. Penn Square Bank was an oil and gas lender that overextended itself, and during the late '70s and early '80s it generated a tremendous amount of business to out-of-town banks that had invested in the oil and gas industry. So when the boom busted, it busted big in Oklahoma City.

After I got back to New York I put together the combination of seeing my child take his first steps on my home soil, and wanting to get out of New York, and wanting to write a book, and realizing that the bank failure wasn't just a local story but one that had national resonance. I spoke to William Shawn, the editor of *The New Yorker*, and then I went back to Oklahoma to check the story out. What I realized was that I didn't know anything about oil and gas, I didn't know anything about banking, and I didn't know anything about this specific bank. But I knew there was definitely a big story there. However, there was no point in my trying to ask questions at that time. You have to gauge your subject matter and know when it's time to ask questions.

Back in New York, I spoke to my wife and we decided to move to Oklahoma City for a year and a half. When I got out there I wasn't ready to ask questions for several weeks because I had so much stuff to read. Then I just started following the story. Even though it was about a bank failure and about oil and gas and involved a lot of technical information, it was ultimately a story about people. I never could have done it if the characters hadn't been so excessive. They were flamboyant, they were unapologetically greedy, and that suited me fine. (The book, which first ran as three long articles in *The New Yorker*, was called *Funny Money*.) That was a case where it was important to be a careful listener. I really understand how people talk in Oklahoma—or at least how they sound. That vernacular is very familiar to me:

> I liked Murray, although he talked a bit too much, and I liked him *because* he talked a bit too much. You could stay as along as you pleased at Denny's; the waitresses just kept pouring the coffee. Murray started out in the Bronx or someplace like it, but he had been in Oklahoma enough years so that his monologues contained frequent pauses, which were followed by the statement "Now, mister, I'm

gonna tell ya somethin'," whereupon he would launch into a parable full of local color and universal implications. When I called him to make a date I would always ask how he was and he would always say, "Well, sir, I'm still short and I'm still chubby."

One morning Murray's lecture began, "In the past, we have had irresponsible borrowers, and in the past we have had irresponsible lenders, but what we had here, and are having to witness the consequences of in profusion, is the meeting, for the first time, of the irresponsible lender and the irresponsible borrower. Any bank that lends money to Poland is nuts. Any bank that lends to Yugoslavia is nuts. Anybody who lends a billion dollars to Mexico is out of his ever-lovin' gourd. And you know what is at the bottom of this? An irresponsible government. The guys who ran Penn Square weren't born mad killers. They were a symptom." Oklahoma's oilies, in other words, were just a bunch of semi-domesticated third-world borrowers.

Those Oklahoma City bankers invented a transaction called the negotiable cocktail napkin. The banker would literally sit in the bar with the customer and agree to lend him a million dollars, and he would scribble something on a napkin. There was no basis for the loan. On one level it was contemporary history I was writing. But that was the easy part, because I'm comfortable writing about people. So if I know that J.D. Allen and Cliff Culpepper and Bobby Hefner are colorful characters, the reporting becomes a straightforward process of following your nose. That's the stuff I love to do— just call up so-and-so and talk to him about J.D. or Cliff or Bobby.

What was more of a challenge, and in a way more gratifying, was learning in detail about the oil business, which is the business my father was in. It was also a business I had never previously understood. Who knows what my motivation was in writing that book? I think it was a whole bunch of things. I really wanted to understand my father, and it was a nice experience to have those oil and gas operators explain the mechanics of how they did what they did. It pleases me that the book has since been used as a textbook in business schools.

Subsequently I wrote a profile of Errol Morris, which became a more serious piece than any I'd written before. Morris was the filmmaker who made *The Thin Blue Line*, which, as he said, was the first murder mystery that actually solved a murder. He had gone to Texas to make a film about the death penalty—about capital punishment—and he ended up finding a prisoner, Randall Adams, who, like most prisoners, said, "I really didn't do it. I'm innocent." Morris found him credible. He discovered that Adams, who had been sentenced to death for the murder of a Dallas policeman, was in fact not the murderer, and he got the real murderer to more or less confess to him on film. The movie sprung Randall Adams. It was the instrument in freeing a wrongly accused man.

Errol Morris had read my book *Funny Money*, which was set in the Southwest, and this film he was working on was also set in the Southwest. He approached me with the idea that I might write about Randall Adams. But the more he told me about Adams and the fact that he was making a movie that became *The Thin Blue Line*, the more it seemed to me that *he* was the journalist who was writing this story. So it would have been silly and redundant simply to write Randall Adams's story. But Morris himself interested me. This went back to my root preoccupation, which is with people. Errol Morris was such an idiosyncratic person that I ended up writing a profile of him that breaks neatly in half.

The first half is a classic profile, a description of him and certain scenes in his life—the basic biographical stuff—until it reaches the point where he gets involved in the Randall Adams case. The second half is about what happened when the film was released, not long after which Adams became a free man. I flew to Texas for the court hearings that settled the case and reversed the guilty verdict, which had been the result of a cover-up among Dallas law-enforcement officials. With Errol Morris I got involved in what became a life-and-death matter. That was a case where I had to stay with a story for as long as it took. I've spent my career at *The New Yorker*, and the magazine hasn't always tried to be topical. Today it puts an emphasis on timeliness. But there must be a recognition that certain things simply can't be rushed.

At one point my profile of Morris dealt with some of the unfinished business in his career:

> Morris still had plans to complete "Dr. Death"—the movie he had intended to make before the Randall Adams case sidetracked him. ["Dr. Death" was James Grigson, a Dallas psychiatrist who specialized in testifying for the prosecution in Texas capital punishment cases.] He also hoped to direct "The Trial of King Boots," a feature-length examination of how an Old English sheepdog named King Boots—the most highly decorated performer in the annals of show-dog competition—became the only canine in Michigan history to be prosecuted, in effect, for homicide. Morris already had a vision of what the film's publicity posters would say: "Only Two People Know What Happened. One Is Dead. The Other Is a Dog."
>
> If Morris could find time to finish "Dr. Death," he might at last tie together an odd mélange of material: interviews with Dr. Grigson himself; action shots of a lion tamer; scenes from lab research on a mammal called the African naked mole rat; archival footage from an Edison silent film called "Electrocuting the Elephant," and a meditation on Zoar, an extinct utopian community in Ohio. After a trip to Europe, Morris had told me with satisfaction about finding the right music to accompany the Zoar material. "It's called the 'Yodeler Messen,'" he said. "I'd been

hearing this stuff on the radio in Zurich, and then I went into a record store and asked whether they had any liturgical yodeling. They came up with 'Yodeler Messen.' It's, like, based on the idea that God might be hard of hearing."

Because that profile was so bound up in Errol Morris's deeply ironic view of the world, it wasn't a drastic departure for me. It wasn't as if I said, "I've stopped being funny and now I'm becoming a social crusader." On the other hand, in 1992 I did write a thoroughly serious piece about someone in prison, Brett Kimberlin. It dealt with a violation of rights and an abuse of power at the federal level. Kimberlin, who was then still in prison in Tennessee, revealed during the presidential campaign in 1988 that he sold marijuana to Dan Quayle in the early '70s. When that story began to break, he tried to hold a press conference at the federal penitentiary in Oklahoma, where he was then incarcerated. Instead he was put in detention—what you or I might think of as solitary confinement—on three occasions. His longest detention occurred just before Election Day and lasted a week. As a result, the story about Quayle and drugs, whether or not it was true, was one that the public didn't get to hear.

I heard about Kimberlin in the early summer of 1992. He had been cooling his heels in prison all this time, although trying hard to get himself out, meanwhile suing the government for what had been done to him in 1988. When I came upon the story it had been reported in *The New York Times*, but no one had put together a comprehensive portrait of who this guy was. There's a tendency to believe that if someone is in prison he is inherently not credible. Somehow a politician is credible. Dan Quayle had always said, through his staff, "The Vice-President has never used drugs. He has never attended a party where illegal drugs have been used, nor does he have any friends who have ever used illegal drugs," which is a remarkable accomplishment for someone his age.

So here we were in 1992, and we had a candidate in his mid-forties running for President on the Democratic ticket, and everything he had done as a young man was being thrown in his face. Yet Dan Quayle, in 1988, hadn't had to answer for his own alleged drug use because Kimberlin had been silenced. I decided to pursue the story because it seemed like a worthwhile thing to do. I made no attempt to be humorous. The narrative had a strength and a gravity of its own that required a clear-cut distance; I knew I should just stand back and let the facts speak for themselves. I gathered hundreds of facts, which I then had to assemble into a chronology. It was complicated stuff, quite intricate. I had to build a brick wall out of these facts. I had x number of bricks, each one a fact, and to understand how certain things happened in 1988 the reader had to understand how *other* things had happened, eighteen years earlier. It was less of a profile than my other pieces, though I did definitely render a portrait of Kimberlin. It was simply an American story.

One other problem with writing profiles is knowing when to stop interviewing the subject's friends and connections. You know it when you start to hear particular character descriptions or anecdotes for the second time. Sometimes I delay interviewing certain people, even though I know they're important sources, until I've done most of the writing, because I sense that the person will tell me something I'll be able to drop into the piece exactly where I need it. But first I want to build the frame of the house and put up the Sheetrock.

In my profile of the magician Ricky Jay, I had a lot of material about the very knotty problem of exposing magic. This is something my subject is absolutely opposed to; he doesn't share information about how a trick works or how he creates a particular effect. He may confide in two or three colleagues, but there are things he doesn't share with anyone. These guys all carry something to the grave. It's what that profile is about—making secrets immortal, which is a wonderful notion, an extremely rich topic. So I waited until the very end to call Steve Freeman, one of Jay's closest friends, and he told me an anecdote that I just laid into the almost finished piece. It was as if there had been a spot sitting there waiting for it all along.

The anecdote caught the essence of what Ricky Jay is about, and it ends with Freeman describing something astonishing that Ricky had done, something that caught him completely off guard. Freeman says, "Did I figure it out? Well, I was fooled at the time. I felt stupid, but it was nice to be fooled."

POSTSCRIPT

WILLIAM ZINSSER • Writing about a place isn't one of the specialties represented in this book; it turns up only in the last two chapters, as a component of nature writing and regional writing. But of course it's a major component of almost all journalistic writing. Everything happens somewhere, and readers want to know what that place looks like and feels like and what's distinctive about it.

Mark Singer's reporting is so strongly grounded in people that we may forget how strongly it's also grounded in the locale that those people inhabit, especially when that locale is his native Oklahoma. "Surveying the Oklahoma City landscape now," he writes in *Funny Money*, "you would hardly assume that oil production had been declining for such a long stretch and had reached such a low level. In the suburbs, where there are two taco joints for every tree, you see wellheads surrounded by high fences in undeveloped residential zones, you see pumping units in strip-shopping-center parking lots. Four-story derricks straddle the wells on the grounds of the state capitol and the governor's mansion, and it matters very little that so many of the wells are just barely oozing crude—that the derricks' main function is to provide a remembrance of things past. Appearances count. Mythology counts."

The lively mixture of human and local detail in Mark Singer's work is a useful reminder that people and places are intertwined in good nonfiction writing—more closely than reporters sometimes remember when they go out on a story and come back to write it. Faced with the need to describe a town or a village or a natural wonder, they fall back on descriptive language, using words like "nestled" and "bustling" and "enchanted," which have long since lost their ability to enchant. One way to keep from sliding into that bog of platitudes is to seek out the men and women who live in those nestled towns, or who work on bustling Main Street, and to get *them* to say what makes their place unusual. You'll usually find them both thoughtful and eloquent.

I struck this rich vein a few years ago when I wrote a series of articles that evolved into a book, called *American Places*, about 15 sites that have become American icons, such as the Alamo, Mount Rushmore, and Yellowstone Park, or that embody a powerful idea about the American dream, such as Mark Twain's Hannibal, the Wright brothers' Kitty Hawk, and Dwight D. Eisenhower's Abilene. Very little of the book's emotional content comes from what *I* wrote about how those places looked and felt to me; most of it comes from what their custodians told me when I asked them why *they* think so many millions of tourists make a pilgrimage to their site every year. For example:

> "A great many people continue to come to Mount Vernon as if it's a pilgrimage," its curator, Christine Meadows, told me. "The shrine aspect of George Washington's home has been important to visitors since the 19th century. That's an especially powerful force at houses where the grave is on the grounds, like Mount Vernon and Jefferson's Monticello. During the 19th century the room that evoked the most moving expressions was Washington's bedroom, because that was the death chamber, and the 19th century was preoccupied by death—there was that Victorian gloominess that descended on people. Today visitors are more interested in the dailiness of Washington's life. They want to know: 'Did he own that?' or 'Did he sit in that chair?' People desperately want heroes and models, and there's a reaching out to connect with objects that Washington used."

> "For most skaters the rink at Rockefeller Center is a release from whatever is going on in their lives," said Carol Olsen, the rink's manager. "They go into their own dreamland. Their faces express oblivion—they're having that one

moment of fantasy. When you were a child there was always something you didn't get to do, and skating is one way of living out that dream. Girls imagine that they're Dorothy Hamill—they'll go out in the middle and do their little spins. Parents and grandparents tell me, 'I haven't been here since I was eight—I can't believe I haven't been back in all this time.' They feel that it's their rink, and they're trying to repeat with their children what they remember doing long ago."

Most Americans come to the falls as a family, said Ray H. Wigle of the Niagara Falls Visitors and Convention Bureau. "They wait until the kids are out of school to visit places like this and the Grand Canyon. They say, 'This is part of your education—to see these stupendous works of nature.' On one level today's tourists are conscious of 'the environment' and the fact that something like this has a right to exist by itself—unlike early tourists, who felt that nature was savage and had to be tamed and utilized. But deep down there's still a primal response that doesn't change from one century to another. 'I never realized it was like this,' I hear tourists say all the time, and when they turn away from their first look at the falls—when they first connect again with another person—there's always a delighted smile on their face that's universal and childish."

What's important about a place usually goes well beyond its location and its appearance. The reporter's task is to find the *idea* of the place. Remember, when you're laboring to state that idea in your own words, nudging the reader with significance, that if you are curious about people, as Mark Singer is, they will often do the job for you.

LAWRIE MIFFLIN covered the New York Rangers for eight seasons, first for the *New York Daily News* and then for *The New York Times*. Between those two stints she spent a year as associate producer of "Howard Cosell's Sportsbeat." At the *Times* she was a sportswriter for two years and deputy sports editor for five years. She covered the New York Cosmos during the Pelé years and has covered almost every sport except pro football, including the Olympics in Montreal, Lake Placid, Los Angeles and Seoul, enjoying becoming an expert on such relatively arcane competitions as gymnastics, diving and horse show jumping.

Subsequently she became assignment editor on the national desk and national education editor and then spent two years developing the *Time's* work-life policies—such areas as flexible hours and job sharing. Now back in the newsroom, she is a reporter covering the television industry. She lives with her two sons in Brooklyn, where she has been coaching youth soccer for five years.

7

LAWRIE MIFFLIN

THE SPORTS BEAT

Sportswriting is no different from any other kind of good writing. It has more pitfalls for bad writing than some other fields—a tendency to lapse into clichés—because it's in the nature of covering sports to write about similar events over and over again. But in many new areas that have become the province of the sportswriter—for instance, talking with doctors or trainers who are hiding injuries or not telling you the truth—the main weapon is good reporting. It's a matter of questioning and not taking people's word for things, being skeptical, pursuing it further, asking other people. Those are the tools of a good reporter in any field.

When I started I was surprised at the number of sportswriters who didn't seem to be trained as journalists. That was back in 1976, when I became a sportswriter at the *New York Daily News*. How I got to that point is a long story, but briefly summed up, I entered Yale the first year Yale took women, in 1969. I had grown up near Philadelphia, where there's a lot of interest in women's sports of all kinds, not just golf and tennis. What I played most actively and loved most was field hockey and lacrosse. Not until I went away to college did I learn that this was considered weird by most people—exotic, somehow. Where I came from, for girls to play field hockey was just like for boys to play football.

When I got to Yale I quickly found the athletic department and asked where to sign up for the field hockey team. They were speechless. They didn't know what I was talking about; I could have been asking where to find the shuttle to Mars. So I said, "What do you mean, you don't have one?" That was the first bucket of cold water, the first intimation that my upbringing hadn't been normal—not all girls across the United States knew how to play field hockey. But it made me realize how much I wanted to play. Until then I had taken it for granted that I would play. I didn't think about it as some sort of feminist agenda. Just as I knew that at college I'd probably want to major in history, or that I'd sign up for some class activities, or go to the movies on Saturday night, I knew that I wanted to play.

So I started the field hockey team. By the time I was a senior it was a varsity sport, one of the first three varsity sports for women at Yale. We were proud of that accomplishment, especially because it was a team sport. The other two were squash and tennis, which are a lot easier to maintain because they are individual sports. Then I went to the *Yale Daily News* and said, "Hey, we're a varsity sport now, so I suppose you'll be assigning someone to cover us, like the football team or the basketball team." They said, "No we're not—we don't have anybody who knows anything about field hockey. Don't be ridiculous." And I said, "But that's not fair," so they grudgingly assigned some poor woman who didn't know anything about *any* sport to cover our games. I had to tell her what to write, because she didn't have a clue as to what the game was about. But I was the captain of the team, so *I* couldn't write the articles.

After that season I covered all the other girls' sports, just on principle. We always said "girls" then. That's another way times have changed; we would call them women's teams now. I never intended to be a staff member of the *Yale Daily News* or thought I was going to be a journalist. I wasn't involved with the paper at all, except that I would come in after the games and drop off my story.

But I had a very perceptive and farsighted professor of

history, Duncan Rice, who knew that I intended to go to graduate school and felt that I wouldn't make it through a Ph.D.
program. He didn't think I had the stamina. I was the type
who wrote term papers the night before they were due; I
always did better under pressure. He said, "I know you're
doing this writing for the newspaper. Why don't you think
about journalism?" I had grown up reading newspapers and
The New Yorker and other magazines, and history is in many
ways current events-related; maybe I would like journalism.
So I applied to the Columbia School of Journalism. I didn't
have any credentials except for those sports clippings from
the *Yale Daily News* and a letter of recommendation from Red
Smith, who had taught a writing seminar at Yale.

At Columbia I was exposed to the broader world of journalism. I was still interested in sports, but I didn't think I
wanted to be a sportswriter. I got excited by journalism in
general and by newspaper journalism in particular. When I
graduated I applied for a job at the *New York Daily News*.
There's a lesson in that. The placement people at Columbia
said, "Don't apply to the New York papers or the Washington
papers or the *Boston Globe* or the *Chicago Tribune*. You'll never
get a job there right out of school. You've got to go work in
the boondocks for a while." Several of us said to ourselves,
"What harm could it do? You write them a letter. If they let
you come for an interview it costs you a subway token down
and back." Which was exactly what happened. They let me
have an interview. Then I kept phoning them. Persistence is
very important in looking for a job. And sure enough, three
of us got hired at the *Daily News* and two of us at *Newsday*. So
much for placement advice.

At the *Daily News* I began as a city reporter, which is a
good thing. You should start as a general-assignment or nuts-
and-bolts reporter if you want to learn. I did that for two
years and then, lo and behold, both *The New York Times* and
Newsday assigned a woman as a sportswriter—the hot new
thing. At the *Times* it was Robin Herman and at *Newsday* it
was Jane Gross. (Jane is now the San Francisco bureau chief
of the *Times* and Robin has also done very well, as a freelance
writer and as a health and science reporter at the *Washington*

Post.) So the *Daily News* said, "Hm, maybe *we'd* better do this too." They knew of my interest in sports because I had been trying to get them to cover women's college basketball. Queens College, believe it or not, in the days before women's sports had become as big-time as men's sports, had one of the best women's basketball teams in the country, but because it was a women's sport nobody knew about it. The *Daily News*, of all papers, should have been covering that team—it's a New York City college. That year they were playing in the tournament for the national championship. I had been pestering the paper about them and had written a couple of very short articles. Finally they said, "Do you want to cover sports?" and I said "Yes."

That was in the spring of 1976. Eventually they did send me to that women's basketball tournament, which they otherwise wouldn't have covered. They also sent me to the Montreal Olympics that summer. Some glimmer of enlightenment in the Neanderthal sports department said, "Oh, Olympics—they have a lot of girls there. They have gymnastics and they have swimming and diving, and the United States has girls there who might win medals."

Anyway, I covered the Olympics, which I loved, and that fall the *News* assigned me to cover a team as a beat—the New York Rangers hockey team. Three things were lucky about that. One was that Robin Herman had been assigned to that beat by the *Times*, so there were two of us. She had covered the Islanders the year before. The second was that the general manager of the Rangers was a man named John Ferguson. He was an infamous macho tough guy; as a player he had been known for fighting—an "enforcer," they call it in hockey. But he was a very fair man, and I think he recognized from the start that the Rangers needed to get good publicity in the two biggest papers in the city. If the *Times* and the *News* were going to assign women to cover his team he might not like it, but it wasn't going to do any good to be hostile toward us. He told the team, "As far as you guys are concerned, Lawrie is the *Daily News* and Robin is *The New York Times*. That's all you have to worry about." That set a tone for the players that was lacking for a lot of other sports.

The third lucky thing was that hockey isn't the most popular and celebrated of our sports; baseball and football are. I haven't done a survey, but I'm certain you'd find that the most vicious harassment of women and the most consistent resistance to women reporters has been in football and baseball—football because it's so macho and baseball because it's so traditional. Hockey players, on the other hand, were less spoiled by fame. Also, at that time they were mostly Canadians, many of them from large, stable families that taught sons to respect their mothers and sisters. That helped. Hockey players were for the most part decent to women reporters, and so were basketball players. George Vecsey, the sports columnist for the *Times*, once said the reason basketball players were so accommodating is that they recognized "the back of the bus" when they saw it. Women sportswriters were being treated the way blacks were so often treated, and it wasn't fair.

So off we went, covering all these games, more than 80 games a year—40 at home and 40 on the road, plus the playoffs—writing three stories for every game because of newspaper deadlines. The first edition goes to press around 7 or 8 o'clock, so you have to write something that holds the space for your game story later. That's discouraging, because it just gets thrown out after the first edition, but your name is on it, so you want it to be reasonably good. In that first-edition story, which we call "the early," you write about injuries or about which players are going to be playing on which lines together, because you don't want to waste a good feature story on something that will run in only one edition.

Then, during the game itself, you write something called a "running story," which is for a deadline around 11 or 11:30, so you don't have time to write the whole story, especially if you want to go to the locker room afterward and get quotes. So what you do, period by period, is keep your computer in front of you (when I started, it was your typewriter), and as things happen you write them. It's called "running" because that's literally what it is—a running account of the game. You learn to be very cautious, because as soon as you finish writing about how wonderfully the Rangers are playing and how they're dominating the other team and haven't allowed more than six shots on the goal for two periods, in the third period they'll fall apart and the other team will score six goals. The final score will be 6–4, and you'll have a story that says, "The Rangers lost to the Maple Leafs by six to four last night. In the first two periods the Rangers were great." So you learn to be careful about the tone of a running story. It ends up being very descriptive, very impartial. Those are things you learn the hard way.

Then, as soon as you finish that story, you slap a lead paragraph on top and you run to the locker room to get quotes. Then you come back and you have until your paper's final deadline to revise the whole thing, work the quotes into it, throw out description that's no longer relevant, and readjust the analysis. It's a hard night's work. People would say, "Oh, you're a sportswriter, isn't that fun—you get to go to all the games," as if you just go and sit and watch. In fact, sometimes you miss a play because you're writing and your head is down. You rely on the other reporters to tell you what happened.

That's an interesting subtopic, incidentally—the matter of reporters competing against each other. There are times when you help your colleague, because he or she needs help and you may need the same kind of help two nights later, and there are times when you don't. Beat reporters work that out among themselves, and it's not necessarily a bad thing. What I resented was colleagues who would come up after the mad dash to the locker room and say, "Did you get something from So-and-so?" Well, maybe I did, and maybe it's a pretty good quote and I don't want it in my competitor's newspaper. On the other hand, the coach usually has a press conference for reporters right after the game, and they're all there in a group, so there's no harm done if a reporter is late and you share those quotes. Sometimes the goalie will have made a spectacular save or let in a terrible goal, and everyone is mobbed around him; maybe I was on the outside of the circle and couldn't hear him. My colleagues will say, "Here's what he said." That's O.K. too.

Which brings me to the subject of women reporters in

the locker room. It's far more analogous to situations in life than you might think. The only major difference is that men are often walking around with no clothes on, and some of them don't think strange women who aren't their wives should see them. One obvious solution is to put a towel around your waist. I could never understand why that wasn't more obvious to everyone. If modesty is really the issue you can pull your pants on under your towel and then take the towel off. And there are other solutions. The Cosmos soccer team, which I covered for a number of years, issued terry-cloth bathrobes to all the players. Clearly the issue isn't modesty; it's the whole idea that women shouldn't be in a man's world. It isn't a job for a woman.

So, for me, there was a lot of proving that I knew as much about sports as male reporters, or that I was willing to learn. At the beginning I certainly didn't know as much as the other reporters, or as the players. So my first rule of reporting is "Ask, ask, ask." You may think you're going to appear stupid, but I found the reverse. I found that players respected the fact that I respected them enough to ask and that I didn't assume I knew as much as they did. In fact, I found that the show-off male sportswriter was almost a caricature to players. (There are probably female reporters like that now too.) A player would say something slightly obscure, and the reporter wouldn't ask a question because he didn't want the player to think he was ignorant. Or a player would say something about the number of goals he scored last year, and the show-off writer would say, "Well, actually you scored one more than that. Don't forget the game against Minnesota on February 7. It was the third period, and in fact I think the goalie you beat was So-and-so." And the player would just say, "Oh, yeah," and think: "What an idiot. This kind of minutiae doesn't matter to me; why does it matter to him?" Over the course of time, by asking good questions and demonstrating to the people you cover what kind of person you are, you earn their trust and their respect.

That's where the locker room is analogous to life: prejudice almost always disappears when people get to know each other.

The Rangers had to deal with me and Robin day in, day out—in practice, on airplanes, in hotel lobbies, everywhere. They got to know Lawrie and Robin; it didn't matter much anymore that we happened to be female. Players on other teams, who didn't see us as often, could only see a female sportswriter coming into the locker room, and their reaction was, "This is wrong, get her out of here!" It works the same way with racial or ethnic prejudice or any other kind. There will always be jerks—that's life. There will always be people you can't win over. But if you work hard enough to build respect and learn your craft, people will usually respect you back.

Roger Angell wrote a piece in *The New Yorker* in 1977 that dealt perceptively with the advent of women sportswriters. He noted that for some older male sportswriters, being on the beat was almost like being part of the team; they felt close to the players and very involved with them. When women reporters joined the scene, those men had to recognize that they themselves were more akin to *us* than to the players. When the players categorized people they weren't going to group the male reporters with themselves; they were going to see themselves as the athletes and the reporters as reporters, whether they were men or women.

Angell's piece concludes with Dave Maloney, one of the Ranger players, talking about having me in the locker room. "Lawrie is—well, I *like* Lawrie," Maloney said. "She shoots straight. She's friendly. When she's in here asking questions it's just two people talking together—not a man and a woman, but friends. She's patient, and patient people are better at that job, I think. Lawrie is just like a sister." And I thought: That's great. I don't want to be their girlfriend; I don't want to be their mother. I'd like them to say, "She's like Red Smith"—that would be the ultimate—but what he said was very nice. Angell then asked Maloney about the last time he remembered women coming in the locker room. It was his mother, he said, when he was eight or nine years old, and she had to come to tie his skates. That was also a nice functional analogy. We were there to perform a specific function, and it had nothing to do with sex or modesty or male-female relationships. It had to do with the reporter-subject relationship. I think eventually all players will come around to realizing that.

I want to get back to writing. As I said earlier, I was astonished at first by the number of sportswriters who didn't know basic principles of reporting, like asking a follow-up question. Coaches would say something that you knew wasn't true, or that was hard to believe, and rather than say, "But if you say that, then how can you explain...?" these guys would just write it down and wait for the next pearl from the coach's mouth. There was a lot of "homerism" and "one-of-the-boysism" in sportswriting in the old days, which was being challenged as my generation came along, and I think women helped to dispel that, because we were never going to be one of the boys.

"Homerism" is rooting for the home team—maybe not actually rooting, because no self-respecting sportswriter would admit to that, but at least being partial to the home team and writing your story through its eyes. It's easy to fall into that habit, because many of your readers are fans of the home team and that's what they want to know most about. But in writing an account of a game you have to be more objective, more critical. It's like being a theater critic or a music critic. No matter how much you like the performer, if it's a bad performance you have to say so.

So being a good reporter is as essential in sportswriting as in any kind of writing: getting both sides of an issue, verifying whether what somebody tells you is true, checking things with many sources. Being a good writer is also essential. Good writing is good writing, in sports as in anything else. Sports journalism is fraught with pitfalls—hype and gushing and clichés and adjectives; they are the bane of sportswriting. There's a little test you can do. Read through the sports pages and see how many adjectives you can cross out, how few of them are serving any illuminating purpose. Usually you can convey more about the impressiveness of an achievement by simply describing it well.

If homerism is one extreme, the other is cynicism—a reporter thinking he must criticize everything and know more than the players or the coaches. I do feel that you have to be a skeptic—to challenge what people tell you and trust what you see with your own eyes. But you don't have to be a smart-ass. Players will tell you more and reveal more about what they do and how they do it if they don't think you're a know-it-all, if they think you're willing to learn from them.

In general, there are three types of sportswriting. One category is game and event coverage—the nuts and bolts, the game story you read the next day. Within that category there are subgroups of reporting. The beat reporter who stays with the team all season long (as I did with the Rangers) is supposed to know everything about that team—not just to write the game story but to tell you how the team is evolving, what they're doing right and wrong, whether they're going to trade someone, whether the coach is going to be fired. Various new beats have also come along. The *Times* has a reporter, Murray Chass, who covers baseball as a business: labor negotiations, player contracts, whether franchises are going to move from one city to another, legal issues like the bigotry case involving Marge Schott, the owner of the Cincinnati Reds. That's almost a non-sports beat; it could be a Washington beat or a business beat. Then there's the Olympics beat. Today most major papers have a full-time Olympics or international sports correspondent, because the Olympics have become such big business now and are held every two years. There also are reporters who cover a non-team beat like tennis or golf, going to all the major events.

The second category is human interest and features reporting, under which I would include the sociology of sport, serious issues such as drug or steroid use, or racism. It also comprises articles about individual players that go deeper than the 700-word quick stories that you write to keep up with the team as the season goes along.

The third category is columns. A columnist is an opinion writer; his pieces should sound like what appears on an op-ed or an editorial page. Red Smith was the best. Any column of his that you pick up is worth reading because of his respect for words, his freshness of language, and his humor. But Red

Smith also had opinions. He had something to say in every column; it wasn't only a feature story dressed up with a heading that labeled it a column. So many columnists today are just writing a sidebar to the event they're covering; they don't bring the punch and the insight that Red Smith brought to the form. His style reinforced his opinions. After the infamous Roberto Duran–Sugar Ray Leonard welterweight championship fight in 1980, in which Duran told the referee, "*No mas*," or "No more," ending the bout, Smith wrote that Duran "had to be sick or injured, because Roberto Duran was not, is not and never could be a quitter." He went on to say:

> The Sweet Science is a harsh mistress, and under her cruel rules the deadliest sin is to give up under punishment. The most damning criticism that can be made of a fighter is to say, in the parlance of the fight mob, that he is a bit of a kiyi or that he has a touch of the geezer in him, meaning a streak of cowardice. The fact that no coward walks up the steps and into the ring isn't good enough for the fight mob. It is further required that when his number comes up, the fighter must endure pain and punishment without complaint as long as he is conscious.
>
> "Do you want me to stop it?" Harry Kessler, the referee, asked when Archie Moore was being slugged senseless by Rocky Marciano. "No," Archie said. "I want to be counted out." He was.

Descriptive writing, very important in sportswriting, may be used in all three categories. It's difficult to do. One of my own favorite descriptive anecdotes came from a young hockey player who had joined the Rangers as a rookie. The brief summary of this kid was that he had been drafted very low, in the third round. Many others were chosen before him; he wasn't expected to be a very good player. He was only about 5 feet 11 inches and maybe 170 pounds, and he was a defenseman; in those days it helped to be bigger and stronger. He was also an offensive defenseman, which is to say he liked to make attacking plays; he didn't just stay back and defend. In short, he had a lot of strikes against him, and he was a good story because, despite all that, he made it. He came to his first pro training camp and everybody said, "Oh, he'll probably get sent off to the minors." But in fact he never played a day in the minors until he was at the other end of his career.

He was a rookie when I was a rookie, and I was intrigued with this kid. His name was Mike McEwen, and he came from Toronto, from a big family. His older brother, who had coached him, always told him, "You can do it, you can do it, you can do it." Mike would tell me these stories because I think he saw me as a sister figure; he had two older sisters and two older brothers back home. His mother had died and his sisters were important to him. Being a female reporter with this guy was a help. People often ask, "Is there any advantage to using your feminine side to get a story?" In general I don't think so, but this was an exception.

By the end of his first season McEwen had set a Ranger record for points by a rookie defenseman. That's an esoteric reference, perhaps, but still, there had been a lot of rookie defensemen through the years, and he had scored more points than any of them. Defensemen aren't supposed to score points; it's more important to keep goals out of their own net. But if they also score points it's a good thing, and he was proud of that. One day, talking with him about how he felt about all this, I tried to pull out of him more than just the cliché, "Gee, I never thought I'd make it, and my brother will be really proud of me."

I said, "Tell me about when you were drafted." He was a very confident kid—you would have to be, to have achieved what he did—and I figured he'd say, "You know, I thought I would go in the first round and I was so surprised I didn't go until the third round." Well, instead he said he had been scared. He said it was the first time he ever wondered whether all the things his brother had told him about his abilities were going to be shared by those pro scouts. That was interesting. It was starting to be "good stuff," as reporters say.

Then he told me that before you get drafted you have to go for a physical exam; the selecting teams want to know about a player's height and weight. They tell you to strip down to just your jock and your socks. So he took two pairs of woolen socks and he put two hockey pucks inside each sock, one under the ball of the foot and one under the heel, and he shuffled into the room and stood real tall, and on all the official documents he wound up being listed as 6'1" instead of 5'11". It said a lot about how badly this kid wanted to make it into the National Hockey League.

That's one of my favorite descriptive anecdotes. First of all, as a reporter you have be able to get that story. Then you have to know it's good—that it's interesting and it's going to make a good story. Then you have to write it just the way you would tell it to someone and not go waxing on about "shivering in the other room and gnawing his fingernails," or "pondering what he should do, an idea flashed into his mind." Don't embroider what doesn't need embroidering.

In starting an interview, what I've always tried to do is make the other person comfortable. Ask some easy questions. Ask things you know he's concerned about, that he'll like to talk about, even if it's off the subject you want to eventually get to. A second thing (this seems so obvious, but it's funny how many people it's not obvious to) is: Don't ask a question that can be answered "Yes" or "No" or "I think so" or "I don't think so." Don't say, "Do you think if the Rangers hadn't drafted you in the third round, Toronto would have taken you in the fourth round?" or "Do you think your reputation is such that..." Then the player says, "Yes," or "No, I don't think so." Instead you say, "What do you think they were thinking about you when you were about to be drafted?" In other words, an open-ended question that will force the person to tell you a lot, rather than just "Yes" or "No."

Ira Berkow, a sports columnist for *The New York Times*, once told me that a successful interview could be conducted, if necessary, with just two questions: "What are your greatest hopes?" and "What are your greatest fears?" (or some variation on them). That's what I mean by an open-ended question. If somebody said to you, "What's your greatest fear?" he would probably get a pretty interesting answer.

WILLIAM ZINSSER • Lawrie Mifflin's account made me nostalgic for the days when reporters covering a game had the modesty to come right out and say who won. Today that news can be a long time in arriving. Half the current sportswriters think they are Guy de Maupassant, masters of the exquisitely delayed lead. The rest think they are Sigmund Freud, privy to the modern athlete's psychic needs and wounded sensibilities. Some also practice orthopedics on the side, quicker than the team physician to assess what the MRI did or didn't reveal about the star pitcher's torn or perhaps not torn rotator cuff. "His condition is day-to-day," they conclude. Whose condition isn't?

The would-be Maupassants specialize in episodes that took place earlier, which they glean by hanging around the clubhouse in search of "color." No nugget is too trivial if it can be cemented into that baroque edifice, the lead. The following example is one that I'll invent, but every fan will recognize the genre:

Two weeks ago Bobby Bonilla's grandmother had a dream. She told him she dreamed he and some of his Mets teammates went to a Chinese restaurant for dinner. When it came time for dessert, Bobby asked the waiter to bring him a fortune cookie. "Sometimes those things can really tell it to you straight," his grandmother said he told Eddie Murray. Unwrapping the paper message, Bonilla saw the words: "You will soon do something powerful to confound your enemies."

Maybe Bobby was thinking of his grandmother's dream at Shea Stadium last night when he stepped to the plate to face the Astros' Doug Drabek. He was 0-for-12 against Drabek in 1993 and was also mired in his longest slump of the season. Nobody had to tell Bonilla that the fans were on his case; he had heard the boos. This would be the perfect moment to confound his enemies. It was the bottom of the eighth, two men were on, and the Astros were leading, 3–1. Time was running out. Could that fortune cookie have been trying to tell him something?

Working the count full, Bonilla got a waist-high slider from Drabek and crunched it. The ball rose in a high arc, and you knew just by watching Bobby that he thought it might carry to the left-field seats. The wind off Flushing Bay was blowing in, but Bobby's "something powerful" was not to be denied, and when John Franco shut down the Astros in the top of the ninth, the scoreboard said Mets 4, Houston 3. Thanks, Granny.

The would-be Freuds are no less eager to swagger before settling down. "Somebody should have told Jimmy Connors that he was into mortality denial before he took the court yesterday against a foe 20 years his junior," they write, experts on player motivation, proceeding to use judgmental words like "predictably futile" and "ridiculous"—no proper part of a sportswriter's vocabulary—to show their superiority over an athlete having an inferior day.

Red Smith had no patience with self-important sportswriting. He said it was always helpful to remember that baseball is a game that little boys play. That also goes for football and basketball and hockey and tennis and most other games. The little boys—and girls—who once played those games grow up to be readers of the sports pages, and in their imagination they are still young, still on the field and the court and the rink, still playing those games. What they want to know when they open their newspaper is how the players played and how the game came out. Please tell us.

MELINDA BECK, a senior editor of *Newsweek*, joined that magazine in 1978, soon after graduating from Yale. She became a writer in its National Affairs section, chiefly covering defense, aviation and social issues, and more recently has been an editor in the "back of the book" section, overseeing such areas as justice, medicine, education, religion, space and the environment. She has written more than 25 *Newsweek* cover stories, launched its award-winning Aging section, and has won more than a dozen journalism awards. She lives in New York with her husband and two children.

JANICE KAPLAN, now senior editor of *TV Guide*, has been a contributing editor to *Vogue* and *Self* magazines, a sports columnist for *Seventeen* and a regular contributor to many other magazines, including *Redbook*, *Cosmopolitan* and *Glamour*. Her five books include the nonfiction *Women and Sports*, two young adult novels and two adult novels, one of which, *Wild Nights*, was an alternate selection of the Literary Guild. She has produced many programs for network and cable television. For five years she was a writer and producer of "Good Morning America," and subsequently she was senior producer of "A Current Affair." She lives in Westchester with her husband and two sons.

8

Melinda Beck & Janice Kaplan

Health and Social Issues

BECK: When I started as a writer at *Newsweek*, not long after college, I was covering everything from politics and plane crashes to murders and municipal finance, and it was a heady feeling, especially because I was so young. I got a rush out of waking up to the clock radio every morning and hearing what was on the news and knowing it was going to affect what time I got home that night, because I was going to be writing about it. That was before I had children, so I had the luxury of working all night, and I did, week after week and year after year, covering some of the biggest hard-news stories.

But the most memorable pieces I wrote during that period were not the *Challenger* explosion or the Tylenol murders. They were articles I just happened to write for the "back of the book"—the feature sections of the magazine. They're still my favorites. One was a report on teddy bears, written largely in A. A. Milne's style, which included a look at the teddy bears of famous people, like Margaret Thatcher. Another was a history of beauty pageants, right after the Vanessa Williams scandal.

I became a convert to "lifestyle" subjects when I stopped writing and started editing. I was given responsibility for the serious part of *Newsweek*'s back of the book—areas such as justice, medicine, science, education, religion and the press. It's an enormous amount of material to cover every week, and usually it had to be squeezed into a news hole that was only about 15 columns, which is five pages in the magazine. I became jealous of all the space the front-of-the-book articles had, when it seemed to me I had the subjects that really mattered to readers—what's happening to their children, their schools, their health, their churches and their courts.

Today the news media are beginning to realize that this is where readers really live. If you look back at *Newsweek's* best-selling covers, except for major events like the Gulf war, they are about subjects like chronic fatigue or arthritis—stories that affect readers' daily lives far more than the latest Washington scandal. My perspective on what's important has changed enormously since I've had children of my own, and I think most readers are facing the same time squeeze. At *Newsweek* we're competing not only with *Time* and *U.S. News and World Report* but with television and VCRs and homework and hobbies and all the demands of everyday life—doing the shopping and getting the kids to bed. People don't have time to sit down and read a really long piece on foreign policy, or even a perfectly crafted piece about what the President did this week. I know *I* don't. When I get a little time, I skip over all that and go to the stuff that I enjoy reading or that's useful to me.

I've been working part time, three days a week, since I had my first child. I've gone back to writing, and in that process I've carved out a new beat on aging. People shudder when I tell them that's my subject. They say, "How can you write about something so depressing?" But I tell them that aging has become a megatrend, and if they haven't already encountered the problems of aging and infirmity and nursing-home costs within their own families, they eventually will.

The aging of the American population is the hottest beat in journalism right now. It's going to create huge changes in everything from health care and housing to work and leisure and family relations. I wrote one cover story called "The Daughter Track," about women who are trying to work and raise their children and also care for their aging parents. Here's and amazing fact: the average American woman will spend 17 years raising her children and 18 years helping her parents. "Helping," of course, can mean many different things. It can mean helping parents to manage in their own home, or preparing meals or arranging transportation for them. It can mean putting them in a nursing home, which doesn't end your responsibilities—it only adds to your guilt and your financial burdens—or it can mean taking aging parents into your own home and rearranging your life to meet their needs. When a parent has something like Alzheimer's disease it's a round-the-clock commitment. The number of Alzheimer's victims in the United States today is 4 million. In 20 years there will be 14 million.

Q. How do writers like you identify these new trend stories, which really are the gut stories of America in the '90s? When do they suddenly become stories? "The Daughter Track" probably wouldn't have been written five years ago.

Newsweek did do a cover story called "Who's Taking Care of Our Parents?" about five years earlier, but that was largely about the phenomenon of people in their sixties looking after *their* parents in their eighties. What's new has been the recognition that women are doing so much of this work, while also shouldering many other responsibilities.

Q. Do you meet resistance from your editors, even when you know you're on the crest of something everybody wants to know?

It's a mystery to me why editors will suddenly leap on a subject. Before that you can talk and talk and talk, and you won't get through to them. It's frustrating if you're a beat reporter who has been following a field for a long time, because the big continuing trends sound old hat to you. But in truth the average reader is just waking up to them. It's the editor's job to sense when the moment is right to do a story, and that may be several years after the experts have started charting the phenomenon.

Sometimes what happens is that you get a great news peg—like the family that abandoned its father, who had developed Alzheimer's disease, at a racetrack in Oregon. That's a perfect opportunity to revisit a number of ongoing issues, like "granny dumping" or the demands of caregiving. As a beat writer you're constantly on the lookout for pegs like this, which give you a chance to take a new look at an old problem.

At other times a publication simply decides that it's going to have a commitment to a particular issue. Then all the old news standards—What's new here? What's the peg?—go by the board because the editors just say, "Dammit, this is important. Our readers ought to know." Often what happens is that somebody your editor in chief rides the train with in the morning has said, "This is really important—you should do a story on it." I remember that we got the green light on "The Daughter Track" because our editor's sister, who was taking care of *his* parents, started beating up on him. He suddenly realized what the whole situation was doing to her and the fact that as a man he was largely escaping it. That got him interested.

Editors are also constantly watching what the rest of the media are covering, and that affects their decisions more than they would like to admit. Menopause recently became a hot topic, not just because the oldest baby boom women are hitting that time of life but because *Vanity Fair* ran Gail Sheehy's long piece on the subject. Significantly, they didn't put it on the cover; they would never run anything that depressing on the cover. But the article got a tremendous reaction—the issue sold out, and women who heard about it were looking everywhere for a copy. Suddenly a topic that nobody had written much about or even dared to discuss became a media event, because it raised all kinds of provocative controversies over hormone replacement therapy and cancer risks and other medical quandaries. *Newsweek* jumped on the story, and we timed it to appear the week Sheehy's book was published, because we knew that the subject would be in the air again. We sold a lot of magazines that week, and Gail Sheehy's book was a best-seller for months.

Q. Do you feel an obligation to write about these stories in a balanced way?

I do, because I grew up in the world of newspaper journalism, where balance is a virtue. It's one of the things they teach you in journalism school, or at least they used to. Today I notice a strong trend away from that and into more opinionated writing. Magazines like *The New Republic* and *Washington Monthly* are mostly collections of essays with a strong point of view. *Newsweek* isn't like that yet, but we're doing far more signed columns and fewer of the big symphony pieces, where you weave in comments from everyone. We're watching our competition closely, and we recognize that what people want to read is changing. By the time you get *Newsweek* you've probably already heard the top of the news that week, and you want a different spin on what happened. In 1992 most of our election coverage consisted of four dueling columnists offering their own take on the political news. In the old days such pieces would have been four sidebars around the main story. Now they *are* the main story.

Q. Would "The Daughter Track," for instance, end by saying, "Here are five possible ways to get some relief for this problem?" Or would the menopause piece advocate one treatment over another?

I try to stear clear of making calls in cases like that, where there's real controversy. Most of the things I write about are debates and continuing battles. That's what makes them interesting, but it also means that there are probably no easy answers. Sometimes we try to give our readers helpful information—maybe a list of community services, which they might not be aware of. But a lot of our coverage is just wringing our hands: "Oh, what a terrible situation this is. Why doesn't the government do more? Here's why: because it costs so much, or the fixes would create even more problems." Maybe that's a cop-out, but I don't like to pretend I have answers when I don't. Often the best I can hope to do is present an issue and let readers come to their own conclusions.

KAPLAN: My approach is just the opposite of Mindy Beck's. She starts with a subject; I start with an ideology. Working for a magazine, she will report both sides of the issue. As a freelance writer, I tend not to do that. I always take a position. I write best when there's a subject I care about, because then I can write with passion. I think that accounts for some of the success I had after I first graduated from college. I wanted to use my writing to open people's eyes—to make them see things in a new way. Specifically, I focused on women and sports. As it happened, sports wasn't a subject I had followed very much. But I wanted to write about women and their lives and their possibilities. That subject *did* matter to me.

I used sports as a way to talk about women and women's issues. In sports, issues come alive. It's hard to write a general article that says, "We need to treat women fairly because they can be as good as men." But it's easy to say, "Hey, here are the facts: Women are running the marathon almost an hour faster than they did ten years ago!" That means something. It's a specific fact from which you can draw a conclusion and make a point. I could have found four experts who would say, "Yes indeed, if women do x, y and z they can be just as strong as men." Instead I used the facts to demonstrate what women can do. Sports became a metaphor—a way to talk about women's abilities.

Eventually I became a contributing editor at *Vogue*, and

"sports" turned into "fitness and health." But I didn't want to lose my ideological slant. One story I particularly liked came about because I wanted to do something about courage. Courage is one of those stories you can't write about in the abstract. I couldn't sit down and write an essay on courage unless it was about a particular person. Various names were suggested to me, and finally I chose one that sounded right— a woman in Birmingham, Alabama, named Barbara Ingalls Shook, who lost a leg and half her pelvis to cancer and then took up skiing. In my article I talked about the specific details of how she managed that. Then I got to draw the conclusions I had wanted to write about in the first place, in a paragraph that quotes her as saying, "A lot of people become obsessed with thinking about what's wrong. I look at how fortunate I am. I lost a leg, but I still have my life."

It's hard to write about someone like that without getting sappy; you're always on that line. And I truly was entranced by this woman. It happened that on the day before my sched-uled early-morning flight to Alabama to meet her, I sprained my ankle. When I woke up at 5:00 A.M., the ankle was badly swollen. I looked at my husband, who happens to be a doctor, and I said, "Honey, I can't go." He said, "You're going to write an article about a one-legged woman who skis and you're going to cancel because you have a sprained ankle?"

So I wrapped up my ankle and found a cane in the attic and went to Alabama. I'm sure Mrs. Shook didn't understand the empathy I had for her, but every time she mentioned how embarrassing it was to have one leg, or to be disabled, or how she thought people were staring at her, I wanted to say, "It happened to me in the airport this morning; I know what you mean." In my article I tried to tell a lot about this woman. But she herself wasn't finally the point of the article. The point was expressed in a sentence that said: "While courage is usually thought of as physical bravery—climbing a mountain, running a marathon—you don't have to be fearless to be courageous. You need a spirit that refuses to yield, no matter what the circumstance."

Q: Both of you, in your work, are very dependent on experts. How do you develop those contacts?

KAPLAN: First, it's important to do your own research. Experts are very important, but you quickly come to understand that you can find experts who will argue either side of a point. So you do all your interviews and you end up with a stack of conflicting quotes, and you have to decide how to use them. That's where I get back to the idea of adopting a point of view—using your writing to make a point. Readers get confused if you say things like, "Some experts question Dr. Smith's findings." Your job is to help the reader along. If you've done your research and you've got your facts you can present a coherent point of view—but not *every* point of view. You want to be fair, but you also need to be selective. The First Amendment doesn't give every quack the right to appear in your article.

Q. How about the biases of experts? Do you find that doctors or scientists or researchers have an ax to grind? How do you guard against that? How do you learn who you can trust?

BECK: The same experts do come around again and again; we call them "the usual suspects." But we consult these people intentionally because they talk in nice, crisp, quotable sentences. They also have short titles. When you're writing a very short piece there's nothing worse than having to call someone the "assistant associate professor of medicine and political philosophy at the University of California at Berkeley, visiting at the University of Texas."

KAPLAN: And, "Oh, can you mention my book?"

BECK: Some of them won't even talk to you unless you plug their book. (That's usually the first thing to go, however, when you're tight for space.) As for knowing who you can trust, you never know completely. But the more you cover a field, the more you know where certain experts are coming from—what special interests may be influencing them. For our menopause story I attended a press luncheon where a well-known expert on hormone replacement gave a speech. The luncheon was sponsored by a drug company that makes estrogen pills. That expert wasn't necessarily on the company's payroll; she had done her own research and had concluded through her own practice that estrogen replacement is an excellent thing. But you always have to wonder: *Am* I hearing the whole story?

That's why I tend to shy away from telling readers what they should do. For every expert like the one at that luncheon, you can find ten women who have had horrible side effects from taking hormones. At this point in medicine there's no single answer about hormone therapy—except that every woman has to weigh her own symptoms and her own family history.

Sometimes I've found so many dueling experts that I couldn't figure out anything concrete to say, and I just stopped dead in my tracks. I've done a lot of writing, for instance, about infertility and miscarriage and all kinds of experimental treatments and theories. What's tough about those stories is that it's often hard to tell how much is even in dispute. Every expert you interview is convinced that his own little research angle is the definitive answer and the other guys are all wrong. Who should you believe? It really doesn't do the reader a service to say, "Here are six answers and nobody agrees."

Q. You mean you just drop the story?

BECK: Yes. Until things become clearer.

KAPLAN: Early in my career I found that in writing and writing and writing about these issues I created my own backlash. I spent years writing about how women should be more involved in exercise and sports, at a time when that subject wasn't being talked about much, until one day my editor at *Vogue* called and said she wanted an article on how women were exercising *too much*. So I wrote an article about how we've become fitness-crazed. But the reason I'm telling you this is that there are many ways you can end up saying the same thing. In that piece I was still making the same point as when I was telling women to exercise more:

> When it comes to their bodies, many women feel that nothing is too much. At various stages of our collective history we have done everything from wearing tight corsets to starving ourselves—all in pursuit of the perfect shape. We generally ignore the question of how this search for beauty affects our health—until it's too late. The current emphasis on fitness and health would suggest that we have moved beyond vanity and embraced more worthy goals. It would be nice to think that we are all exercising now because it's good for us. But it can't be forgotten that definitions of beauty change, and the ideal woman is depicted now as lithe and powerful, her body pulsing with just a hint of muscular definition. To match that image we are excercising with a vengeance. Athleticism has been glamorized, and we are devoting ourselves to jogging and weight-lifting, aerobic dance and calisthenics, squash and swimming.
>
> All this is a dramatic switch from just a few years ago, when women trapped in sedentary lives suffered from the weak muscles and saggy forms that no amount of dieting could alleviate. This is ample evidence that exercise helps regulate weight, improve health and increase muscle tone.... But the compulsive exerciser bears far less resemblance to Billie Jean King or Grete Waitz than to the traditional woman who spent hours preening in front of a mirror. Athletes work to get their body functioning at its best, but the exercise-obsessed are driven by very different motives. They yearn to be shapely, and since sports are now fashionable they accept them as a means to their goal.

The point I wanted to make was that what matters is how you feel about yourself. If we've just changed one image for another—if we've changed from looking like Twiggy to look-

ing like whoever's muscular and great-looking, like Madonna—
then we haven't gotten very far. As a writer I think it helps
when you really believe something. The traditional advice to
writers is: Write about what you know. I say, write about what
you really care about, what really moves you.

Q. Do you consider self-esteem one of your beats?

KAPLAN: In many ways it is. Self-esteem is one of those
women's-magazine subjects that they run every six months or
so as a cover article. But as a writer you try to find new ways
to talk about it. I wrote one piece on "social phobia," which
was a new term to me. It was coined to describe people whose
shyness goes over the line. The piece was called "I Want to
Go Home." It was an interesting subject because it was mostly
about women and self-esteem—about successful people having fears about going to a party, or facing a room, or whatever.
I did a lot of research by going to different groups, including a
meeting of the American Psychiatric Association, where I
could interview many psychiatrists. Ordinarily I don't write in
the first person, but I couldn't resist starting this article:

> Here I am in San Francisco at the annual meeting of
> the American Psychiatric Association, doing research into
> social phobia, and I don't want to leave my room. It's not
> that I'm afraid to leave, but there are 20,000 overeager psy-
> chiatrists down in the convention center, and being with
> them is exhausting. My hotel room, on the other hand, is
> quite peaceful, complete with a thick terry-cloth robe and a
> very large bathtub. The psychiatrists I am avoiding con-
> sider this an early symptom of social phobia.

Lately I've noticed that many magazines are more interested in letting the writer's own voice come through; strict
reporting isn't quite so necessary. A few days ago an editor
called and asked me to do a piece. It wasn't a magazine I had
written for, and I said, "Well, I'm not sure I know your magazine's style well enough to do it." And she said, "Don't writ

in our style—we're looking for new voices." That was refreshing. They may not like it when they get it, but at least there's a recognition that good writing has its own voice.

Q. That's why your lead on that social phobia piece is good. Readers identify with you up in that hotel room, and they'll hang around for whatever serious point you want to make.

KAPLAN: I took a similar approach in an article called "Public Pregnancy." My premise was that I have two children, that I love having two children, but that I hated being pregnant. The ideological point I wanted to make was: Why is it that when you're pregnant, people feel they have a right to your body? Everybody can touch your stomach and say, "Oh, it's going to be a boy," and when I went out jogging, people would say, "Don't do that, it's dangerous for the baby." All of a sudden I became public property.

Q. What was the tone of the piece—mild outrage?

KAPLAN: Yes, but it also was: Here's what you can do about it. And it was also: Why is it that everybody felt it was O.K. to tell me not to jog but nobody ever gave me a seat on the bus?

Q. One thing that interests me about the work of both of you is that you're ahead of where the country is. There's a dearth of ideas until a writer looks ahead and says, "Aging is a story," or "Fitness is a story." You have to be more risk-taking or prescient than other writers. Aren't you both to some extent leaders of opinion?

KAPLAN: We're writing on subjects that touch hearts and lives and people's sense of who they are. I hope we're taking risks and I hope we're making people think.

WILLIAM ZINSSER • One day in the mid-1950s I glanced up from my desk at the *New York Herald Tribune* and saw a curious figure being escorted across the huge city room toward the corner office of the executive editor, George A. Cornish. The visitor was a small man wearing a shabby black overcoat and a black hat, who looked as if his job might be to stamp passports at the airport in Bogotá, and he was carrying a very long black box.

Word soon got around that his name was Louis Azzaraga, that the box contained a secret camera that could take panoramic pictures, and that he had been hired by Ogden R. "Brown" Reid, then the president and editor, to enliven the paper with what came out of his "camerama." Sure enough, over the next few weeks the *Herald Tribune*'s pages—including the front page, long an ornament of American typography— were dismembered to accommodate, stretching across eight columns, a view of 40 or 50 blocks of New York skyline.

There was no journalistic reason for running the pictures. They conveyed no information that readers couldn't obtain with their own two panoramic eyes. Nor were they notable as art; the paper's own photographers did far better work every day. What the pictures had was one undeniable trait: they were very wide. After a while the owners realized what everyone else knew all along—that there isn't much demand for very wide pictures—and Louis Azzaraga vanished as abruptly as he had come. Nobody ever did see what was in the black box.

Anyone might suppose that this dalliance between the paper and the panoramist was one of those accidents that happen in the best of families. But it was no accident. Louis Azzaraga was just one entrant in a long parade of conjurers and mountebanks whom the Reid family embraced in the belief that quality wouldn't be their salvation but gimmickry might. With a succession of cheap features that they hoped would lure the masses away from the *Daily News*—sleazy gossip columns, a green sports section, a pop "Early Bird" edition and other patronizing novelties—they steadily eroded the character of their paper and drove many of its best editors and writers and readers away. (The masses also stayed away.)

I had joined the *Trib* in 1946, when it was considered the best edited and best written paper in America, and I quit in 1959, when it was far along in the decay of body and soul that, in 1966, would kill it. In 13 years I watched its standards become lower than my own. Much has been written about why the *Herald Tribune* died, and the reasons are usually financial: the rising cost of newsprint, the tough demands of nine different unions, the tightening grip of *The New York Times* on retail advertising, the inability of the city to support two papers that appealed to the same class. All true—death was finally caused by too much money flowing out and not enough coming in. But there was another flow that was no less fatal: the constant departure in sadness and despair of men and women who knew what they were doing and the constant arrival of hucksters who didn't.

When I came home and told my wife that I had resigned from the paper where I had expected to stay all my life, she said, "What are you going to do now?" It was a fair question, I thought, especially as we then had a one-year-old daughter. I said, "I guess I'm a freelance writer," and that's what I was, for the next decade. At that time it was still possible to be a generalist in America, writing for general-interest magazines, and at first I wrote a number of articles for *The Saturday Evening Post*. Then the *Post* died. Then I wrote a column for *Look*, and *Look* died. Then I spent five years writing pieces for *Life*, and *Life* died; my editor called one afternoon and said, "Whatever you've got in your typewriter, send it to somebody else." My journalistic past is littered with the bones of dead publications, but I don't take it personally. Writers should live in the expectation that they will wake up some morning and find their bosses gone.

The writer's job, finally, is to go it alone and keep breaking new ground. Listening to Mindy Beck and Janice Kaplan, I heard a persistent theme: as reporters tracking social change in America, they are far ahead of their editors. Janice Kaplan, early in her career as a freelance writer, was one of the first journalists to force editors to recognize that the limitations they placed on women's physical abilities were the result of the editors' own limited vision. In the piece about marathon runners that she mentioned in our class, which I remember well, she noted that after the Boston Marathon was opened to women, in 1972, women improved their running time in the next dozen years by 50 minutes, while men's times improved by only a few minutes.

"This dramatic progress," she wrote in *Vogue*, "should begin to answer the question of training vs. hormones. Are women slower and weaker than men because of built-in biological differences, or because of cultural bias and the fact that we haven't been given a chance to do what we can do? ... Whether the gap will ever be closed seems almost beside the point. What matters is that women are doing what they never dreamed they could do—taking themselves and their bodies seriously." What also matters is that editors of women's magazines started taking women's bodies seriously. Writers like Janice Kaplan gave them the word.

Melinda Beck, beating her head against *Newsweek*'s resistance to her news that aging has become a crucial subject to millions of readers, said it was a mystery to her why editors "will suddenly leap on a subject. Before that you can talk and talk and talk, and you won't get through to them. It's frustrating." Her story raised so many "Amens" in our class that she had obviously struck a bitter truth. Several students, speaking from experience as freelance or magazine staff writers, cited as a major obstacle the fact that bosses move to their own unfathomable rhythms. One student later said to me, "If you ever do a class on the internal biases of editors and how they affect news coverage, count me in."

ROGER COHN, after starting his career as a reporter on several Eastern newspapers, became a staff writer for the *Philadelphia Inquirer*, where he covered urban affairs and was among the first journalists to make a beat of local environmental issues. He received an Alicia Patterson Foundation fellowship to study the federal public housing system, and he reported extensively on inner-city housing problems. He has written articles for *The New York Times Magazine*, the *Washington Post*, *Audubon*, *Outside* and many other magazines. He is now executive editor of *Audubon*. He lives in Brooklyn with his wife, Patricia Leigh Brown, and their two sons, Jacob and Gabriel.

9

ROGER COHN

NATURE AND THE ENVIRONMENT

As an editor of *Audubon* magazine, I'm reminded every day that nature isn't as simple a subject as it once was. Writing about the natural world in the pristine tradition of Emerson and Thoreau is a luxury we can no longer afford. Today the domain of the nature writer includes nothing less than the whole environment and all the social and chemical and biological and political issues that are involved in its destruction and its protection. It's an important and even an urgent beat.

That sounds obvious now. But as recently as 15 or 20 years ago there were very few environmental writers on American newspapers. I know because I was one of them, and the attitude of most editors was "That's just a fringe issue." I was a reporter on the *Philadelphia Inquirer*, covering environmental and pollution issues in the Philadelphia area and other parts of the country—stories like the toxic disaster at Love Canal—and trying to find a way to make these new issues understandable to the general reader. What I always tried to do was to find the people story beneath the environmental story.

At Love Canal I wrote not only about the scientific studies of the toxic dumping but about the psychological effects on families who lived in the neighborhood. In Montana I wrote about a dispute over coal mining on the adjacent reservations of two Indian tribes. The Northern Cheyenne were dead set against any mining development; it violated their land, and they were fighting the coal companies. But the Crow, on the next reservation, were eager to get the money and the potential jobs that were being offered, and they were wooing the coal companies to come in and strip-mine their lands. I tried to tie all this together with traditions of the two tribes that went back to Custer's last stand, when the Cheyenne were attacking Custer's troops and the Crow were Custer's scouts. So although it was an environmental story—a strip-mining story—it was also a people story. The two can't be compartmentalized.

Yet good environmental writing doesn't come out of nowhere. It comes from the tradition of good nature writing. And some of the best nature writing, in turn, has been done by people who weren't nature writers; they just wrote beautifully. So I'm going to start by reading you a few passages by three of those beautiful writers. Here's the first one:

> I still keep in mind a certain wonderful sunset which I witnessed when steamboating was new to me. A broad expanse of the river was turned to blood; in the middle distance the red hue brightened into gold, through which a solitary log came floating, black and conspicuous; in one place a long, slanting mark lay sparkling upon the water; in another the surface was broken by boiling, tumbling rings, that were as many-tinted as an opal; where the ruddy flush was faintest, was a smooth spot that was covered with graceful circles and radiating lines, ever so delicately traced; the shore on our left was densely wooded, and the

sombre shadow that fell from this forest was broken in one place by a long, ruffled trail that shone like silver; and high above the forest wall a clean-stemmed tree waved a single leafy bough that glowed like a flame in the unobstructed splendor that was flowing from the sun. There were graceful curves, reflected images, woody heights, soft distances; and over the whole scene, far and near, the dissolving lights drifted steadily, enriching it, every passing moment, with new marvels of coloring.

I stood like one bewitched. I drank it in, in a speechless rapture. The world was new to me, and I had never seen anything like this at home.

That's by Mark Twain, from *Life on the Mississippi*. I started with that because I think it shows clear, vivid description of the natural world. It's based on careful observation— good reporting. It describes how the scene affected the writer, without being hackneyed or corny—not an easy task. And the writer, Mark Twain, isn't known as a nature writer.

Here's the next one:

There was no fat on [the land] and no luxuriance anywhere; it was Africa distilled up through six thousand feet, like the strong and refined essence of a continent. The colors were dry and burnt, like the colors in pottery. The trees had a light delicate foliage, the structure of which was different from that of the trees in Europe. . . . The chief feature of the landscape, and of your life in it, was the air. Looking back on a sojourn in the African highlands, you are struck by your feeling of having lived for a time up in the air. The sky was rarely more than pale blue or violet, with a profusion of mighty, weightless, ever-changing clouds, towering and sailing on it, but it had a blue vigor in it, and at a short distance it painted the ranges of hills and the woods a fresh deep blue. In the middle of the day the air was alive over the land, like a flame burning; it scintillated, waved and shone like running water, mirrored and doubled all objects, and created great Fata Morgana. Up in this high air you breathed easily, drawing in a vital assurance and lightness of heart. In the highlands you woke up in the morning and thought: Here I am, where I ought to be.

That's from *Out of Africa*, by Isak Dinesen. The book begins, "I had a farm in Africa," which you may remember from the movie—Meryl Streep's voice saying with a phony Danish accent, "I had a farm in Africa." But despite that, it's lovely. It has a personal element—the feeling of what the altitude means to the person who is breathing it—which is often found in the best nature writing. It also has a strong sense of place. That quality is mainly associated with another nonfiction form—travel writing. But it's also very important in nature writing.

Here's my third example:

The Big Blackfoot isn't the biggest river we fished, but it is the most powerful, and per pound, so are its fish. It runs straight and hard—on a map or from an airplane it is almost a straight line running due west from its headwaters at Rogers Pass on the Continental Divide to Bonner, Montana, where it empties into the South Fork of the Clark Fork of the Columbia. It runs hard all the way. . . . From its headwaters to its mouth it was manufactured by glaciers. The first sixty-five miles of it are smashed against the southern wall of its valley by glaciers that moved in from the north, scarifying the earth; its lower twenty-five miles were made overnight when the great glacial lake covering western Montana and northern Idaho broke its ice dam and spread the remains of Montana and Idaho mountains over hundreds of miles of the plains of eastern Washington. It was the biggest flood in the world for which there is geological evidence; it was so vast a geological event that the mind of man could only conceive of it but could not prove it until photographs could be taken from earth satellites. . . .

The straight line on the map also suggests its glacial origins; it has no meandering valley, and its few farms are mostly on its southern tributaries which were not ripped up by glaciers; instead of opening into a wide flood plain near its mouth, the valley, which was cut overnight by a disappearing lake when the great ice dam melted, gets narrower and narrower until the only way a river, an old logging railroad and an automobile road can fit into it is for two of them to take to the mountainsides.

It is a tough place for a trout to live—the river roars and the water is too fast to let algae grow on the rocks for feed, so there is no fat on the fish, which must hold most trout records for high jumping.

That's from Norman MacLean's *A River Runs Through It*. I chose it not only because of its feeling of place but because of the way MacLean describes the natural environment of the valley—its geology, how it was formed. That material could have been so dry; believe me, I've seen other pieces that were submitted to *Audubon* describing rivers like this. Instead of saying it's a narrow valley, MacLean says that the only way a river, a logging railroad and an automobile road could fit in the valley was for two of them to take to the mountainside. It's full of graceful phrases.

Having a passion for a place is crucial to this kind of writing. At *Audubon* we started a column called "A Sense of Place," and we received pieces from pretty good writers that had nice description and all the necessary facts. But often they didn't tell me why the writer cared about the place—and therefore why I, the reader, was supposed to care. Which you can't say about those last two pieces. One other major element in writing about the natural world is the natural life that inhabits it—animals and birds and fish and plants. That, too, is often done badly—it's terribly purple or overly academic. The trick is to get the scientific detail right and still bring the writing alive.

Audubon, which started in 1887, pioneered this kind of nature writing in magazines—the kind I've just been reading to you—and it upheld the tradition for almost 100 years. But by the mid-1980s there was a feeling among many readers that the environment had become a mainstream issue—it was no longer a fringe issue—and that it was now part of the national agenda. Today we therefore try to make the magazine more issue-oriented, more current, and we get a little impatient with writers who send us stories that totally ignore the environmental factors behind those stories.

We got one piece, for instance, about the Florida Keys, by an old-time nature writer. He went down there and took a fishing trip and wrote about how the fishing isn't as good as it used to be and how there are too many people. I said to him, "Let's get some science in here. You wrote that there aren't as many manatees. What happened to them? Let's make some calls." We found out that the manatees, mammals that swim close to the surface in the waters of southern Florida, are being killed off by motorboat propellers and that a proposed refuge for them was in political trouble. The writer also said he missed the days when Key deer were plentiful—that's a species unique to the area. A little digging revealed that a refuge had been set aside for the deer, which are an endangered species, but that they were coming off the refuge because tourists and newly arrived residents were feeding them, which is illegal. Hundreds of the deer were being killed on the roads. Those are issues that just can't be left out of a piece about how the Florida Keys aren't what they used to be.

Another submission was by a writer who had gone on a birding trip to the King Ranch in Texas—an organized tour. The ranch is a huge tract of land, hundreds of square miles, and he wrote that it has a lot of wildlife that's very beautiful. It was a nice little piece that might have worked for *The New York Times* travel section. But that's not our province. I said to the writer, "This is pretty interesting. How many other ranches are doing this?" Well, it seems that protecting wildlife has become a big business on these big Texas ranches.

Ranchers used to shoot as predators any wildlife that got in the way of their cattle. Now they're finding that they can make more money by having tours come and look at birds and mountain lions. It turns out that in Texas there's more protected acreage on these private ranches than there is on federal or state land. It made a good story. It was a positive development, just as in the Florida Keys the issues were negative. But both articles finally came down to the need for solid reporting. That applies to this field as much as to any other.

We've just run a piece about a town in Louisiana called Morrisonville, which has literally been wiped off the map. Dow Chemical was polluting it so badly that, rather than cleaning it up, they just bought the whole town. Some families didn't want to sell, but eventually they settled with Dow and agreed to move. It's an amazing story—about people and the loss of their community. And it's a story for *Audubon* because it illustrates that what we as a society do to the environment eventually affects people and their communities. We don't exist in isolation from the natural world; what we do to the air and water and wildlife eventually affects us all. For instance, our magazine is doing a piece now on lead poisoning in inner cities—not exactly a nature story, but very much our business.

We're also doing in-depth articles on issues that aren't the traditional territory of a nature magazine. One piece that we're working on now, for instance, looks at whether environmental protection necessarily means the loss of jobs, or whether more jobs can be created through new businesses and technologies that protect the environment. Such issues simply can no longer be compartmentalized as business or economic stories. They are also *our* stories.

The best kind of article for us, I think, is one that is both a good nature piece and a good issue piece. One of my favorite examples was written by Sue Halpern, who isn't a nature specialist; she's just a really good writer who appreciates the natural world, and I called her to see if she would do something for us. The subject we settled on was the Aransas National Wildlife Refuge, on the Texas Gulf Coast, which has been a protected wintering ground for the whooping crane since it was created by President Roosevelt in 1937, when the total number of whooping cranes in the world was down to 29 and the bird was on the edge of extinction. Trying to save it was a very big cause of the conservation movement in the '30s, and this year's record total of 40 nesting pairs is regarded as a milestone in the birds' recovery. But I had heard that they were being afflicted by some kind of disease, and I asked Sue to go down there and take a look. She found that the main threat to the birds was not the disease. It was the dredging of the Gulf Intercoastal Waterway, and her story turned up a whole web of interrelated issues, as environmental stories so often do:

Because the cranes at Aransas are the last of their species in the wild, they are vulnerable to a single catastrophic event—a hailstorm or a hurricane. This is not fanciful. In 1940 a flock in Louisiana lost half its birds to a hurricane, and the other half never recovered, which is how the birds in Texas came to be the linchpin for the survival of the species. But now, due to the steady erosion of their winter habitat, the pin is coming loose.

"We are losing between one and four acres a year, two hundred and thirty so far," says Tom Stehn, the biologist at Aransas. According to his calculations, 15 percent of the cranes' habitat at Aransas has been chipped, sawed, sunk and washed away since the early 1940s, when the U.S. Army Corps of Engineers, under the authority of Congress, dug a channel between the refuge and the barrier islands that protect it from the Gulf of Mexico. The channel is just one small section of the Gulf Intercoastal Waterway (GIWW).

"The GIWW was put where it was to protect boat traffic from wind and high seas. It's the right project in the wrong place," says Johnny D. French, senior staff biologist for the Fish and Wildlife Service in Corpus Christi. Boat waves pound the shoreline, causing it to break up and dissolve. In some places the 210-foot channel is now 400 feet wide.

The article goes on to describe how various agencies tried to address the problem. The Fish and Wildlife Service came to the U.S. Army Corps of Engineers, citing the erosion statistics and the Endangered Species Act. In reply, a biologist for the Corps of Engineers cited the limits of its authority. "We want to make everyone happy, including the birds," he said, "but our mandate is to maintain the shipping channel until Congress tells us not to." At that point the Sierra Club Legal Defense Fund, representing the National Audubon Society, threatened to sue.

That's typical of the complexity of an environmental story in the 1990s, as more and more interested parties get involved. The crux of the problem, Halpern writes, is that whenever the Engineers dredge the channel to maintain a 12-foot clearance for ship bottoms, they have to dump the "spoil" somewhere, and over the years this has resulted in massive landfills—"levees that reach the sky"—on land opposite the Aransas Refuge that the cranes used for feeding. The writer then puts the cranes' plight in historical perspective.

What happened when the Army Corps of Engineers first built the GIWW and buried the whooping crane habitat with spoil is a microscopic version of what has happened to the birds since pioneers pushed west across the plains and some of them stopped to settle there. As grasslands were tamed into croplands and ponds were drained, a landscape that had been hospitable to the whooping crane became alien, impossible territory. Eventually the cranes, which once nested in North Dakota, Illinois, Minnesota and Iowa and ranged from the Arctic Circle to central Mexico, were restricted to a narrow 2,600-mile corridor between Texas and Canada's Northwest Territories.

Even within Aransas, only about 8,000 of the 47,261 acres are flat enough, and wet enough, to sustain the cranes. These are the acres that are washing away. Whooping cranes are territorial birds that typically live with a life-long mate on 230 to 1,000 acres. But as total acreage diminishes and the flock increases in size, individual territories are shrinking.

That's helpful history. But there's still one more constituency to be heard from—one that figures in many environmental stories today—and that's the concerned citizen. Sue Halpern, riding on a boat that takes bird-watchers through Aransas, which has 389 species of birds, more than any wildlife refuge in America, gives her story a human dimension that makes it memorable:

The deck officer Steve Birk takes the microphone and points out tiers of concrete sacks, impaled on metal rods, lining the shore. "Those bags are not for decoration," he says. "They're to reinforce the bank. The Army Corps of Engineers dug the channel, but they didn't seem to want to come back to fix it. So a bunch of us got together and started the Shoreline Project. The bags cost two dollars apiece and weigh ninety-four pounds, and if you donate a few bucks we'll lift one over our heads and throw it down in the mud and yell your name out loud."

The Shoreline Reclamation Project that Birk is talking about is one of those unlikely partnerships of people who, on most days, would have nothing to say to one another—or worse. Under the joint direction of volunteers from both the Corps of Engineeers and the Fish and Wildlife Service, hundreds of individuals, from office workers in Corpus Christi to waitresses at the local crab shack to longshoremen to Steve Birk and Captain Ted Appell, donate materials and equipment and two days in June to bolster the eroding coast with bags of cement and slabs of concrete matting.

"We heard that they needed a way to get the materials up to the Aransas, so we said we'd do it," says Billy Harper, manager of Hollywood Marine in Corpus Christi, whose barges and tugs have delivered tons of concrete to the refuge each year for the shoreline project. "Other companies furnish steel rods and hammers and filter cloth. It's hard work standing in the mud in the middle of the summer with the mosquitoes, lifting hundred-pound sacks of wet concrete. But people do it. They come the first day and then, unbelievably, they show up the next day, too."

The capacity of whooping cranes to elicit such a human response is not only historical; it accounts for their remarkable ability to survive other human activities, like land development and water diversion and hunting. In 1945 the United States Whooping Crane Project, a joint venture of the American and Canadian governments and the National Audubon Society, initiated a public education campaign to teach hunters and others along the whooping crane flyway to recognize the birds and understand how near to extinction they were. People were encouraged to count the birds, which numbered around 17, not to shoot them. It was this campaign, and all the newspaper stories and editorials it engendered, that is credited with making the whooping crane one of the best known and most beloved of endangered species. . . . As wildlife exists in nature, and as nature is delicately balanced, so the whooping crane is a symbol of how easy it is to lose a species, even one that is protected and popular, not out of indifference but from an inability to recognize how things are connected.

That's an environmental story that has everything—including, by the way, some nice nature writing about the cranes. Of its journalistic challenges is that it has no villains. Everybody has the best intentions; even the Corps of Engineers people are sensitive to their responsibility to an endangered species, as well as to the government. The writer's obligation is to report the story in a balanced way.

Of course many environmental stories do have villains. But even then we want the writer to report the story and tell it in a compelling way, without becoming an advocate. We ran a very powerful piece on the residue of strip-mining in Appalachia, by a writer named Ted Williams, who, I think, is the best example of someone who bridges the old outdoors type of good writing with good natural history and good hard reporting. In 1977 a landmark strip-mining law was passed that was supposed to clean up all the abandoned strip-mine sites. Mountains had been gouged out, and toxic run-off from the exposed rock and soil was flowing into streams, so that thousands of streams, especially in West Virginia and Kentucky, were badly polluted. That 1977 law was such a big victory for environmentalists that everyone thought—I certainly did—that the clean-up procedures were working.

Well, Ted Williams called me one day and said, "You know, nobody talks about it, but that law has cleaned up very little, and illegal mining is still going on down there." So I asked him to go to West Virginia to take a look, and his article began by describing the severe damage he saw that was being caused by the unreclaimed pit of the F&M Coal Company:

> As strip-mines go, the F&M pit is not especially large. But along with its two partially revegetated sister mines, it is a world-class producer of sulphuric acid and toxic metals—800,000 gallons of run-off per day right into aquifers, wells and the left fork of Sandy Creek, now fishless for at least six miles. The F&M pours into Tygart Lake—a 1,750-acre jewel that supplies drinking water to Taylor County, plus smallmouth and largemouth bass, walleye, channel cats and panfish to anglers from all over America. The buffering capacity of the lake is being used up. . . .

None of this was supposed to happen after the law was passed in 1977, Williams writes. He found that operators have consistently circumvented the law by forming companies under phony names that skim off the profits from their mines. Then, when it's time to clean up the stripped land and treat the acid drainage, they declare bankruptcy and take their money and disappear, with their assets protected. They leave all this damage to the environment, and nobody is accountable. Our writer broke that story.

Williams's piece wasn't advocacy journalism, although it did criticize the Office of Surface Mining in Washington. It pointed out that the legislation was passed during the Carter administration but that Reagan was President by the time it could take effect, and during the Reagan and Bush years the office was stocked with people from the coal industry who didn't enforce the law strictly. In his article Williams writes a damning indictment of the director of the OSM, Harry Snyder, a former lobbyist for a railroad that was a heavy investor in coal. But *Audubon* isn't like *Sierra*, which is very much an advocacy magazine—its viewpoint is the viewpoint of its parent, the Sierra Club. At *Audubon* we take a journalistic approach—we talk to people on all sides of the issue. In the care of the article I mentioned earlier, about Dow Chemical buying out that town in Louisiana, our writer spent a week talking to a lot of people in the area and at the Dow plant. The result was a fine, hard-hitting piece of reporting that considered the views of all sides but also told how a pollution problem ultimately destroyed a community.

When we started doing these stories we heard from a number of old *Audubon* readers who said, "What became of the nice nature magazine we used to love?" And we did lose some of those old readers. But now we're attracting new readers—young people who thought the old magazine was a little stodgy. And there's one other development that has come as a pleasant surprise. A readership survey showed that *Audubon* has a very high percentage of readers in their 50s and 60s—a much higher percentage than the industry considers safe for the future of a magazine. But it turns out that many of those older readers also thought the old magazine was getting tired, and they're excited about what we're doing. Those people are committed, and they'd rather read a piece that tackles environmental issues than just a nature piece. Many of them are activists themselves.

POSTSCRIPT

WILLIAM ZINSSER • Not long after Roger Cohn became a senior editor of *Audubon*, in 1992, he called and asked if I would write a piece for the magazine. I told him I wouldn't. "That wouldn't be right for me, or for you, or for *Audubon*," I said. I'm a fourth-generation New Yorker, my roots deep in the cement. I've never accepted an assignment that I didn't think I was suited for, or didn't feel comfortable with, and I'm quick to tell editors that they should look for someone else. Roger Cohn said—as good editors should—that he was sure we could think of something, and a few weeks later he called to say that *Audubon* felt it was time for a new article about Roger Tory Peterson. Was I interested? I said I didn't know enough about birds.

But not long afterward I happened to see a PBS television documentary about Peterson, and what seized my attention was that Peterson was still going at full momentum at the age of 84, painting four hours a day, making arduous field trips, and photographing birds in habitats all over the world. That *did* interest me. Birds aren't my subject, but survivors are— how old people keep going. I remembered that Peterson lives in a Connecticut town not far from where we go in summer. I could just drive over and meet him; if the vibrations weren't right, nothing would be lost except a gallon of gas. I called Roger Cohn and said I'd be willing to try something informal—"a visit with Roger Tory Peterson," not a major profile.

Of course it did turn into a major profile, because as soon as I met Peterson in his studio I realized that to think of him as an ornithologist, as I always had, was to miss the point of his life. He was above all an artist. It was his painting that had made his knowledge of birds accessible to millions and given

him his authority as a writer, editor and conservationist. I
asked him about his early teachers and mentors—great American artists like John Sloan and Edmund Dickinson—and
about the influence of the great bird painters James Audubon
and Louis Agassiz Fuertes, and my piece became an art story
and a teaching story as well as a bird story, surprising and
engaging me on many levels. It was also a survivor story; at
84, Peterson was on a daily schedule that would tax a 50-year-
old.

The moral for journalists is: Think broadly about your
assignment. Don't assume that an article for *Audubon* has to
be strictly about nature, or an article for *Car & Driver* strictly
about cars. Push the boundaries of your subject and see
where it takes you. Bring some part of your own life and
learning to it; it's not *your* version of the story until you write
it. When you do, try to find some personal connection with
your subject at the outset. Write a lead that tells your readers
why you're the person taking them on the trip.

In my case, finding such a lead was difficult. I had never
written anything about nature. How could I make myself
credible to *Audubon*'s readers as a guide? Finally (as it often
does) memory came to my rescue:

> For many years our family has had a summer house on
> the shoreline of southeastern Connecticut, overlooking a
> tidal marsh that has a generous allotment of egrets and
> herons and other wading birds. We also have a returning
> population of ospreys, which nest on the tall poles that
> people who live along the marsh have built to help them in
> their tenuous recovery from near disaster caused by DDT.
>
> Among those native waders and divers, one day about
> 30 years ago, somebody spotted a flamingo, its gaudy pink
> plumage an affront to New England reticence, and we all
> hurried down to marvel at it and at whatever miscalcula-
> tion had brought us a tropical bird that we didn't think got
> much farther north than Hialeah. Someone notified *The
> New York Times*, and the *Times* in turn called Roger Tory
> Peterson, who lives in a nearby town, and asked him to

take a look. Peterson came over and certified our visitor, and the *Times* ran an article the next day, along with a picture of a flamingo. It wasn't our flamingo; it was a photograph from the files, but only another flamingo would have known the difference. In any case, there would be no doubting of the story itself—the *Times* had gone to the high priest.

Since that summer day I've often enjoyed knowing that we live in the same part of America as the man who made America a nation of bird-watchers, his *Field Guide to the Birds* a best-seller since 1934; for many families, looking something up in Peterson is as habitual as looking something up in Webster. Recently my enjoyment took a new turn when I watched a PBS documentary called "A Celebration of Birds," which summed up Peterson's life and work. It had so much beauty and accumulated wisdom that I wanted to know more about him—how he spends his days and what he thinks at the age of 84. He agreed to a visit, and when we met I asked him if he remembered our flamingo. He said he did. How, I asked, did he think the stranger had gone so wrong? "Birds have wings," he said, "and they use them."

All writing is a journey that begins with an invitation. Having finally hit on a way to introduce myself to an audience of bird lovers, I felt that I could relax and proceed with the trip, confident that they would tag along.

JOHN S. ROSENBERG began his career as a writer and editor for the Conservation Foundation in Washington. Moving to New England, he wrote a weekly piece for the Connecticut section of *The New York Times*, covering the state's business and economic news, and thereafter was a free-lance editorial consultant to corporations and nonprofit institutions. He has written articles for the *Columbia Journalism Review*, *The Progressive* and other magazines. From 1991 to 1994 he was editor of *Vermont Magazine*, where his special passion, he says, was to engage journalism in the public issues facing Americans today. In 1995 he was appointed editor of *Harvard Magazine*. He lives in Cambridge, Massachusetts, with his wife, Susan Bennett, and their two daughters, Alyssa and Eva.

10

JOHN S. ROSENBERG

LOCAL AND REGIONAL WRITING

What we're trying to do at *Vermont Magazine*—and what all good regional or community journalism is trying to do—is to provide quality coverage that's of interest to people who live in the region or are interested in it in a significant way.

So if you look through our magazine you'll find the usual reader service material, like restaurant and inn reviews, plus a column about crafts, a big enthusiasm in Vermont. We also cover such obvious areas as art and culture, nature and the outdoors, and interesting people. Finally, we intensively cover economics and politics, the hard social and public policy issues in the state—subjects that we think really matter to Vermonters' quality of life. That doesn't make us *The Saturday Evening Post* reincarnated. But it does mean that we—and other good regional and city magazines—can range widely in search of subjects within our little geographic niche.

In our September/October 1992 issue, which had nice coverage of the leaves because 800,000 people come up to look at fall foliage, we also had a very long article on mental-health care. We try to treat our readers as full people—to cover the issues that appeal not just to their hearts and stomachs but to their minds. We thought that if the magazine treated people as serious, engaged adults it could find 50 or 60 or 70 thousand of them who would buy it, which is all we need to survive.

We do all this in a way that's different from covering hard news. We're not doing daily newspaper journalism or wire-service journalism; we're not *Newsweek* or *Time*. We're bimonthly, and for us a fast-breaking article is four months. On articles that deal with environmental issues or health care or education reforms, we never care about what's going to happen to a particular bill in a particular legislative committee next week. We're writing articles that will establish the issues for readers for an entire year, or two years, or five years. We prefer writers who can stand back from the daily machinations of policy-making and look at larger questions, such as: "Will the reform of Vermont schools produce smarter students?" We'll try to find out. To me that's an enduring kind of journalism. It's also a lot more fun to write and to edit.

Q. When you say your intent is to "establish" an issue for your readers, do you mean you're writing about these issues before they actually break?

We try to do that. In 1991 we commissioned a big article on health care. The reporter and I agreed that an article on "health care" would take 100,000 words and nobody would read it or understand it. But when we looked at health care in Vermont we saw that the state has one great big hospital and 15 little ones, and that those little hospitals are going to go out of business because the funding of health care is changing rapidly and they don't have any modern technology. Still, they *do* have a role to play—to take patients in and stop the bleeding and send them somewhere else. So when those little hospitals begin to cut services, or to close, people will be up in arms. Therefore our article on the changing status of Vermont's rural hospitals was a way to get at all kinds of problems about changing health-care delivery.

As it happened, the magazine came out a few days after I had waited to have breakfast with the governor, who had just died of a heart attack. His successor is the only governor in the 50 states who is a doctor, and when he took office he immediately said he was interested in health-care reform above all else, so our magazine looked incredibly timely.

We've done the same thing with education reform and with Vermont's environmental laws. In each case, I've asked the writer to look at the big picture. Knowing it's going to take us so long to publish the article anyway, we cross our fingers and hope that the legislative policy-making process will be as slow and as cumbersome as it usually is. So far it has made us look like geniuses.

The kind of journalism I'm talking about isn't confined to the microscopic magazine that I run. You'll find it in any of the country's good regional magazines and even in some of the airline magazines. It's a staple of *New York* and *Milwaukee* and *Texas Monthly* and of the Sunday magazine in newspapers like the *Boston Globe*, *The New York Times* and the *Philadelphia Inquirer*. This means that as a writer you have a lot of places to look. You don't have to say, "If Tina Brown [of *The New Yorker*] doesn't buy this query, I'm dead."

Which brings up a related point: I view our medium—regional and community and city publications—as a good one for taking risks. That's healthy for writers. My advantage is that I am the editorial staff of my magazine, so all the mistakes are mine. This isn't one of those magazines where the writer gets a letter back saying, "Three of us like it, three of us don't like it, and three of us can't decide." I try to answer all queries the day I get them. When I've made mistakes—rejecting something too hastily—and the writers have come back to me, we've gotten some fine writers out of that process, partly because they know who they're dealing with. That's always to a writer's advantage.

Although I want to take risks, I also want to make the risk work, so I work closely with writers. If I get a query from a writer who says he wants to write an article about education, I ask: "What *about* education? Who are you going to interview? What approach are you going to take?" I want to see samples of the writer's published work, and when we have a contract—after he or she has done some research and started writing—I'll probably call up two or three times and say, "How's it going? How's it playing out relative to your query and to your outline and to what we talked about?" Probably I also will have exchanged two or three long letters with the writer.

Then, when the story comes in, I'll probably edit it more intensively than most writers are used to. We may decide to change the lead. We may take the brilliant first paragraphs and make them a sidebar. We may make a sidebar the lead. It's a long process. Most of the writers I've put through the process have stuck with it, and we haven't had to do that kind of work again, so I see it as an investment. It lets our writers, who aren't writing for very much money, know they're going to have a good chance of success, even if it's a risk-taking article. They're not likely to get a letter from the editor saying, "That's not quite what I had in mind."

Part of risk-taking means that magazines like ours not only enable writers to spread their wings. They also give many writers their start. In some issues of *Vermont*, 90 percent of the writers hadn't written for a magazine before, and half of them hadn't done *any* professional writing.

Of course some things go beyond taking risk, regardless of a writer's experience. Let me tell you some of the things I flag when I get queries from writers. Because ours is a current magazine, I turn down all historical queries; we get reams and reams of them. We also get lots of letters from octogenarians with stuff that seems real and current to them but not to anyone else. I've had six queries *this year* about the time Pearl

Buck spent in Vermont; I don't think that would have been interesting then, so it certainly isn't now. We get an incredible number of queries about first-person accounts: "The amusing time my family and I spent at a quaint inn and discovered the cutest antiques store." The trouble with that kind of writing is that it's so often introspective. It's like a diary— there isn't much reporting. Our editorial guidelines for writers include one extremely hostile paragraph about personal submissions.

Q. What does your hostile paragraph say?

It says: "We occasionally use first-person essays where they have a special character and where the writing is of *exceptional* quality. Without meaning to sound harsh, much of the first-person writing we see is just lazy journalism, of far greater interest to the writer than to any reader, so we reject a lot of this kind of material." We also get a surprisingly large number of queries that turn out not to be about Vermont—wonderful stories, for instance, about great places to fish in the upper peninsula of Michigan.

Q. When you're sifting through all those proposals, which ones are going to catch your eye?

The ones that show a lot of work. If I get a query that says, "I think it would be interesting to write a story on what the census says about Vermont," although that might start to interest me, it wouldn't interest me as much as: "The census data will show that Vermont, which everybody thinks of as home-grown and rural, in fact isn't that way anymore. Vermonters go around saying they're the most rural state in the nation and therefore unique. But the census data will show that all the adjoining counties in New York are more rural and less densely populated, and that those counties and the counties of northern New Hampshire and Maine are also less ethnically diverse than Vermont. That changes all the standard assumptions, and that's how I would report it." That's a good example of what I mean by "The writer has thought about it." It's a proposal that led to a story we ran in *Vermont Magazine*.

Finally, I'm always willing—in fact, eager—to take a risk on humor. Vermont is rich in oral, rural humor, but not much of it finds its way to us, and what does rarely survives the transition into print. Instead we often get a poor imitation of the real thing: a writer trying to spin a "story," often in a fake-folksy language and very often with a nasty undertone about the crafty farmer and the "funny" thing his cows do to the naive city slicker who drops in for a chat wearing $250 Italian leather loafers. I've tried to cultivate good writers who can comfortably use humor in their reporting for stories that seem to need it—a state gathering of dowsers, for instance— and the results have been good.

So much for general principles. Let me tell you how we've made them work. When I became editor of *Vermont Magazine* it was well designed, it looked good, and it was well written. But it was more about homes and lifestyles and consumer issues than I thought it should be. What the magazine lacked was the serious journalism that matters to people, and that became my first priority.

For instance, there's a writer named Richard Ewald, who is a classic Vermonter. He's a furniture maker, he makes maple syrup, and he's a writer. He writes on crafts, and he's done some good cultural pieces and profiles of artists for us. One day he came to me and said he wanted to write about mental-health care in the state. He had never tackled a hard news story, but I said I'd like him to look into it. And he went away.

We have very rigorous deadlines—something is due September 1, plus or minus six months. Well, the "plus six months" had passed, and I called Richard and said, "What's up?" He said, "It's on its way." What arrived was a 50-page manuscript. It had a four-page chronology of mental illness from before Herodotus; I'm not kidding. I threw out all that stuff and took a closer look. Inside the manuscript, completely lost, was a very interesting story about how, 20 or 30 years ago, Vermont had a doctor who became aware of psychoactive drugs and their ability to help people maintain "normal" behavior.

On the basis of that finding he thought the state could be "deinstitutionalized." As a result, what used to be a 2,000-person mental hospital in Waterbury now has 50 patients, and the state is essentially committed to eliminating institutional care. If you threw that many people out into the street in Vermont you would expect a problem. But in fact Vermont has very successful local facilities for these people. I thought that was an exciting story—large numbers of men and women who ought to have psychiatric care have been integrated into the community, as compared to the state hospital, where patients were made to strip to the waist and shovel coal in near-zero weather as therapy.

So we got down to that story. Richard Ewald isn't a policy-oriented man. He's very personal—you can see that in his writing about crafts—and that's the strength of this article. He begins by describing two dangerous escapades by people who went briefly out of control. He then explains that those two people are charter members of Southern Vermont Survivors, a state-financed support group of ex-patients and consumers of mental-health services:

> Like some 3,000 other Vermonters (and about 2.5 million Americans) who experience long-term or serious mental illnesses such as schizophrenia or severe depression, they have also survived nightmarish periods when suicide was an inviting way out. They have survived estrangement from family and friends, loss of employment and financial stability, and the social stigma of mental illness. And they continue to survive the debilitating effects of the powerful drugs that are both a bane and a benefit.
>
> . . . for the past several years Xenia Williams and Will Wilcox have been employed by the same local public mental health organization from which also they receive services in the form of counseling and drug treatment. Wilcox

> is a full-time van driver and foreman of a work crew.
> Williams is an outreach caseworker. This sensible and suc-
> cessful arrrangement . . . demonstrates a truism that many
> might agree with, though few would say it so bluntly: Ver-
> mont may be one of the best places in America to be
> "crazy."

Ewald takes the fear out of the story, and throughout he
maintains that human touch. In his first draft he got hope-
lessly lost in a morass of research. But when we reduced it to
an account of some people working their way through the
system it really worked—and that achievement had never
been reported. In this case, Vermont, which people think of
as a recreational state, has a lot to be proud of.

That kind of article is the guts of every issue of *Vermont*.
We also have commentary—on politics and the economy—in
every issue. It's an extremely difficult kind of writing, but it's
important because it complements our regular service material and helps to explain the world—our part of it, anyway—
to our readers in a fresh way. Of course, America is overrun
with political commentators—there are practically two per
voter. They all have ponderous things to say, but very few of
them can do what we require, which is to write a column that
will stand up for five or six weeks, because that's how long our
closing time is. We have to have a different kind of commentary, written by a different kind of person.

Bill Porter is the former managing editor of a Vermont
newspaper. He's a gadfly. He's from Alabama and now lives in
northern Vermont, and he talks like Demosthenes, with the
stones still in his mouth. But he writes vigorously, in simple
declarative sentences, and he has an earthy voice. In the following column he explains the phenomenon of how Vermont, which has been a state since 1791, which until 1992
voted only once for a Democrat for President, elected a
socialist named Bernie Sanders several years ago as our one
and only member of the House of Representatives. Citing as
a typical voter one highly conservative farmer named Andy, a
Marine veteran of World War II in the Pacific, Porter writes:

*   *   *

Andy cast his ballot [for Bernie Sanders] with enthusiasm. Though he has never been much of a joiner, never had time for causes, Andy thus became part of a coalition that has redefined Vermont politics. [He] linked arms with far-left ideologues, with environmentalists of all stripes, and with organized labor. He signed on with disenchanted schoolteachers and tax-weary wage earners, with the elderly and the young, with activists and dropouts.

These are all members of the Sanders coalition. They don't have much else in common, but they all voted for the winner, and in doing so they sent a message that all future office seekers will ignore at their peril.

As commentary that captures the essence of the election in a fresh way—the fact that it was an "in your eye" kind of vote. It doesn't talk abstractly about new alignments of political power or give us stale observations from a ward heeler or a party boss.

I also hunted down all three of the economists in the state and found the one who could write. We now have a column on the economy that does the same kind of thing. One recent column, on taxes, begins: "How do you spell relief in 1991? Vermont legislators spell it t-a-x-e-s." Not a brilliant lead, but it works and it gets at the readers' big concern: "What does the future hold?" That's what economists are trying to fathom—and what good commentary will tell you.

Obviously I'm proud of how *Vermont Magazine* covers serious issues. But no reader wants those stories as his only diet. So here are some other kinds of stories we work every bit as hard to produce. One of our readers' major interests is the outdoors and nature. Fortunately, probably our best writer is a man named Alan Pistorius, the author of several excellent books on birding and other nature subjects. He has told me that as a child he preferred to play with birds and animals rather than with children. I've been out birding with him, and I'll see something and he'll say, "Well, it's a juvenile something-or-other hawk, but it's missing one of its primary feathers." I'll say, "How do you know that?" He'll say, "Well, the last feather to the left is green." He's an obsessive of the best sort.

When I joined *Vermont Magazine* I found in the files the draft of a story Alan had written on the return of the moose to northern New England. If you ever see a sign that tells you to slow down for moose when you're driving in Vermont, pay attention; hit a moose at high speed and it comes through the windshield. Alan's draft was full of information and was wonderfully written, but there were no people in the entire article. So I said to him, "How about talking to people who have encountered moose?" He said, "Oh, I could never do that." I mentioned a man named Charles Willey, the state biologist who studies moose, and Alan said, "Well, he's a busy man." I said, "For God's sake! Your taxes are paying his salary!" So Alan finally screwed up his courage and talked to Charles Willey and then completed his report on moose in Vermont. I'll read you parts of the lead of his piece and you'll see why I was turned on. Then I'll show you what we've encouraged Alan to do since then, as we've gotten him to treat human beings as another interesting species.

An autumn bull may surpass 10 feet in length and 1,500 pounds in weight; it may stand 7 feet at the shoulder, and may hold aloft a pair of antlers spanning more that 6 feet. Impressive numbers, and this largest of the world's 36 deer does sometimes take the breath away. . . .

Fully exposed to the light of day, however, . . . a moose doesn't look quite right. It strikes one that *Alces alces* is a cold-climate version of the designed-by-committee camel. . . .

For starters, the proportions are all wrong. The great bulky body is precariously supported by stilt pegs, rather like a sumo wrestler's body perched on a ballerina's legs. The beast is front-heavy as well as top-heavy. The large head (too long for its width), massive neck and humped shoulders render the rear quarter comically inadequate. The front end gets all the decoration, too: the donkey ears, the loose pendulous upper lip (which both undermines the animal's dignity and reduces expectations in the IQ department), and, hanging from the throat, the shaggy dewlap (the "bell"), whose sole apparent purpose is to point up the embarrassing inadequacy of the animal's four-inch tail.

There is, in short, a touch of the ludicrous about the moose, which, reinforced by befuddled expressions and a reputation for erratic behavior, undercuts its considerable claims to grandeur. At the same time, it bestows on this oversized deer more personality than most ungulates can boast, rendering it winningly human, as witness its cartoon progeny, the lovable klutz Bullwinkle.

Early settlers of Vermont's forests probably saw moose as neither heroic nor comic personae. More probably they saw them as an unimaginably lucky resource, a kind of mobile food locker.

After the story came in I asked Alan what he would like to do next. "How about writing about mosquitoes?" I said. Vermont has many low-lying flooded fields, where lots of mosquitoes breed. In 1989 they showed up on the nightly network news with Dan Rather, and hotels in the state lost hundreds of thousands of dollars of reservations while the governor and her staff swatted bugs on camera and said, "No, there's not a problem."

So I got Alan to write about mosquitoes, in the course of which he ended up having to talk to people on the local mosquito-control squad; he even went up in a crop-dusting plane. It became a pilgrimage for him, and he started getting quotes. Here's an excerpt from his article. The second sentence is our entrant in what I think of as the *New Yorker* contest between John McPhee and Paul Brodeur to get the longest sentence in the magazine—and believe me, we don't pay by the word:

Art Doty directs the pilot east up over the Goshen plateau to overfly several small, isolated wooded wetlands that have also been found to be heavy mosquito producers. The plane turns back west, and Silver Lake appears suddenly and briefly as a shimmer of sun-glint to our left, and almost immediately we come up fast on what appears to be the end of the world, and over the engine noise Doty shouts, "We're going to give you a thrill!" to the man in the back seat who would rather undergo bowel surgery than be treated to a "thrill" in any aircraft, particularly one the size of a phone booth, and then the plane pitches and lurches and cants as it labors through the crosswinds blowing down the Moosalamoo escarpment, and Doty, a pilot himself, cheerfully shouts, "Nothing safer than these small planes," as we drop dizzily over the blue expanse of Lake Dunmore before leveling off for the return trip to Cornwall, during which the two pilots pass the time chatting about "controlled crashing," apparently a topic of lively interest to spray applicators.

Q. He's flying high here because you've given him confidence. Would he do that for the kind of magazine that has nine editors, three of whom are going to say, "That's not funny," and three of whom are going to say, "What's he doing up in the plane?" Aren't they finally going to end up not running it?

He never cut loose like that before because nobody asked him to do this kind of reporting. It hasn't been his first or even his third instinct to report on the officials who are involved in these issues. But Alan is a good reporter, and where the people and issues interest him, there's no stopping him. As for us, we're delighted to go along for the ride. Editors and readers crave pilots like Alan.

Sometimes I've intervened with the folks Alan has interviewed. He did a piece on milfoil, weedy stuff that looks like an aquarium plant, which is choking all the lakes in Vermont. He and I had elaborate consultations and correspondence with the scientists who are working on the problem, and every time they would object to something in Alan's manuscript he would say, "Should we drop it" and I'd say, "No, we're not going to drop it." I had more correspondence with them than I had with him, but the story's great.

Not that the process always works. I once asked Alan to write about the Vermont Institute of Natural Science, which is a bird research center. He said, "Well, it's an organization of people, and I could never write that." And he won't. I said, "You could write it in your sleep and I'll pay you to do it and it'll be good." But he won't do it. But if you ask him to write about nature per se, he'll cut loose. He's a specialist, and in that context he really loves to spread his wings.

Another category of regional writing is the travel piece: describing a place. It can be a special house, it can be a trip, it can be a profile of a community or a town. We do lots of those pieces, partly because we have to—we have to cover towns all around the state. What we try to avoid is chamber of commerce stuff, which can be cloying if you get someone who's just a booster. We also avoid exhaustive lists of the "27 most important inns you have to stay in." We try to delve into a community and to be sensibly discriminating. Sometimes that's risky, because it's important to talk to people who are established in the community, and those people aren't always willing to say things that might irritate other people. But we've often made it work.

There's an interesting town called St. Johnsbury in the far northern part of the state. It used to have a big manufacturing industry and thriving railroads. Mostly, however, those industries aren't there anymore. It's a diverse community because it has a good private school, which recruits students from Saudi Arabia and Japan and all over the world. The headmaster of that school, Bernier L. Mayo, wrote a profile of the town for us. He's a fourth-generation resident, so he's not writing about the place with fresh eyes, but his eyes are worth a lot to us because he knows the lore of the community. This is an article I don't think we could get from anybody else. It's just a straight-out description of his hometown.

St. Johnsbury is a town of hills. If you walk at right angles from any spot on any of our rivers you will very soon be climbing a hill. There are Sand Hill, Higgins Hill, Hooker Hill, Crow Hill, Clay Hill, Hastings Hill, Harris Hill and Breezy Hill. When I was a young boy I thought "avenue" was another word for hill. We have Eastern, Western, Concord, Parker, Barker, Mountain, Washington, Highland and Boynton avenues—all hills. Despite that, whenever anyone says that some place or someone is "on the hill," he means Main Street, which isn't a hill at all, but a three-quarter-mile plain, the flattened top of the glacial sand dune. The Academy's teams are called the Hilltoppers, not because they are on top of a hill but because the Academy is on Main Street.

Until automatic transmissions replaced standard shifts, the test of a car was this: Could it make it all the way up Sand Hill in high gear? The test of a boy was this: Could he pump his bicycle all the way up Eastern Avenue sitting down? And our bikes weren't the 12-speed marvels that kids ride today; they were one-speed, balloon-tired monsters with only one adjustable part, the seat.

Travel writing is one of the most encrusted and cliché-ridden kinds of writing when it's done poorly. This piece is done very well. It's got a texture and a flavor to it.

Another natural kind of "travel" piece for us is one that describes an institution—a local college, say, or a museum. One thing Vermont has is a lot of self-improvement places, like the Bread Loaf Writers' Conference, or Yestermorrow, which teaches you how to do home construction. All of them think they're incredibly wonderful and incredibly important, and they all think we should write features about them. I was tearing my hair out about this, and then I remembered that we have a young writer named Scott Sutherland, who has written some fine humor pieces for us. So I said, "Here's x amount of money. Go to all these places and write one article that covers them all."

He said, "How should I do it?" I said, "Let's confect an

article in which we say that you went to one place each day for a week to become a perfect person." Of course the research took longer than a week, but what he came back with was a warm, funny piece that gave readers a sense of how people spend time at these institutions learning how to hammer, sail, paint, weave, write—whatever. It wasn't cruel; it was a perfectly fair piece. It was a little personal, but there's no other way to get past the grim, clanking coverage of these places, which are really about self-absorbed people. It gave our readers information and it left them with a smile. None of the schools was terribly offended. (Not that I would have cared.)

Finally, there are stories I can't categorize. They're simply about the place where we live, the place our magazine covers. As a newcomer to Vermont, I've spent a lot of time wandering around, trying to figure out what goes on in the state. Late in the winter of 1991 I was driving to Albany, New York, and I happened to pass a lake that had four or five hundred huts out on the ice. People were ice-fishing, and I thought: That's interesting, all these brightly decorated huts. It's twenty degrees below zero, and each of those people is alone, staring at a hole in the ice. I wanted to write about it for the following winter, and I was in a panic because the ice breaks up in the early spring. Even the people who go ice-fishing realize that it becomes dangerous. So I had to get something done quickly, and I didn't know how. If you knock on the door of somebody's ice-fishing cottage and say, "Hi, I want to interview you," you're likely to get stuffed down the hole in the ice. These people are self-selected to *not* want to talk to you. They spend the winter out there not wanting to talk to their families; they're not looking for reporters to drop by.

On a lark I called up Jerry Gibbs, fishing editor of *Outdoor Life*. He lives in the far northern part of the state, on Lake Memphremagog, which extends from Vermont 25 miles into Canada. Because it's colder up there, the ice stays later. Its other advantage for me, since I want the magazine to get into this culture, is that it's a very French-Canadian part of

Vermont. Jerry said, "Sure. I know these people. I'd love to go out," and he wrote an article that got at this community of absolute nuts—people with names like Jersey Drown and three guys named Souliere, whom I can't tell apart. Jerry can, and what he came up with is an article about something distinctively Vermont—something just right for our magazine—and the very unusual people who make this place special:

> On good days the smelt or perch come fast, and anglers work their holes intensely. On the smelt grounds, ice houses cluster, sometimes only eight feet separating them over the prime fish-holding spots. "Once," Jersey Drown remembers, "I was fishing a flasher, one of those attractor spoons that dart out to the side when you jig it. I hooked up and it was a pretty strong fish. 'Couldn't be a smelt,' I thought. I had pretty light line and fought that fish carefully for maybe half an hour. Over in the next house Ben Smith was fighting a fish, too, which turned out to be me. His flasher had got off to the side and we had hooked each other. He finally got my rig in, saw what it was, hooked a little smelt on and let it go. When I finally got my line in I couldn't understand how that little thing could have pulled so hard so long. Later he told me what happened."

POSTSCRIPT

WILLIAM ZINSSER • I've been following *Vermont* since 1987. That's when David Sleeper, another of my former Yale students, told me he was going to start his own magazine. A good writer himself, he had been managing editor of the Vermont-based *Blair & Ketchum's Country Journal* when its founders sold it to a company in Pennsylvania. He liked the state he was in. "I decided that there was a need for a magazine that would help people who love Vermont," he says. "The only existing magazine, *Vermont Life*, was owned by the state and therefore couldn't or wouldn't deal with controversial issues, such as growth and the environment and overdevelopment, which are the most troublesome issues to Vermonters. It also didn't cover politics. It also didn't accept advertising. So I saw a market need as well as an editorial need.

"I didn't know what a spreadsheet was, or a receivable," Sleeper now recalls, but after two hard years of market testing and money raising, he had the knowledge and the capital to proceed. Since then the economy has given him many wakeful nights. *Vermont Magazine*, born at the end of the prodigal '80s, sailed forth into the depressed '90s, which were particularly hard on receivables in the magazine business. But David Sleeper is his own boss, unlike most journalists, and "putting something like this together," he says, "has been tremendously fulfilling." I salute him for such a creative act of journalism. His magazine has given Vermont a responsible new voice, and it has given writers a home where they could develop their craft under an unusually good and caring editor, John Rosenberg. Such nurturing is the best thing that can happen to a young writer.

When journalism-bound college seniors come to me for

career advice I tell them two things. One is: "Don't think you have to work for a magazine your mother has heard of." The imagined glamour of working for one of the Time Inc. or Condé Nast magazines can in fact mean several years of oblivion in clerical chores. I also say: "If you find an editor you like and trust, try to work for that person, whatever his or her magazine is about." I point out that a newsstand near my office sells well over a thousand magazines, many of them very good, and that somebody has to write, rewrite, edit, copyedit, design, promote and otherwise midwife them all.

One Yale graduate came to New York in 1983 to be an artist. An American studies and art history major at college, he needed a job to support his painting career. I steered him to someone, who steered him to someone else, who sent him to the editor of *50-Plus*, a magazine for people of a certain age, who took a liking to him and hired him as "associate editor." His mother had never heard of *50-Plus*, nor had I, but *somebody* had—its circulation was close to 400,000. The staff was tiny, and so was the pay.

The apprentice soon became a jack-of-all-jobs, acquiring such expedient skills as last-minute editorial surgery, headline and caption writing, working with photographers, planning layouts, and dealing with press agents and press releases. By asking questions he also learned about printing, circulation and promotion. He never patronized the magazine's old-age mentality; he didn't chafe at having to write and edit in his early 20s for readers who were mainly 60-plus and 70-plus. Instead he learned to focus on their probable interests and needs—a good lesson for editors at any age. He wrote one article on how to take your grandchildren through Disney World. Another article advised older drivers on which new cars were best for them. He went to Washington and reported on senior-citizen legislation—bills that were working their way through Congress. Meanwhile he was becoming established as a painter, and he began to write for art magazines about New York artists whose work he found influential.

Two years afterward he left *50-Plus*, grateful for the education, and co-founded a magazine called *The Journal of Contemporary Art*. As David Sleeper had, he perceived a need. Unlike traditional art magazines, the *Journal* carried no art; it consisted of interviews with artists explaining their ideas and their methods. Noting its arrival, *The New York Times* said that it filled the classic role of European coffeehouses, giving artists a gathering place to talk about their work. Handsomely typeset on a computer and desktop-published, it was sold in the bookshops of major art museums and has become a research archive for libraries and university art departments. Early in its launch, lessons learned at *50-Plus* about printing, distribution and postal regulations—subjects presumably not taught in journalism school—eased the editor over many hurdles. At 29, needing more time for his art, he sold the magazine to like-minded young editors, and he is now a successful painter.

I like to think about *Vermont Magazine* and *The Journal of Contemporary Art* and other excellent newcomers that sprang from an individual vision, like *Granta* and *Lingua Franca*, and about editors like John Rosenberg, because amid so much ululation over the death of print journalism and old-fashioned values I see no such mortality. Many magazine editors with old-fashioned values are alive and well in America, and those editors' magazines—magazines such as *Travel Holiday*, *The American Scholar*, *Lingua Franca* and *Audubon*—are the ones I now mainly write for. My articles aren't seen by many people I know, but I'm compensated in a form that's more important to me. I have the pleasure of writing for one editor whose judgment I respect—not for a committee of editors— and of working with junior staff members whom those editors have trained to be punctilious about usage, accuracy and other nuances of shepherding a piece into print.

All eleven of my companions in this book, from the time I first knew them at Yale, had high standards. By remaining true to those standards they have gone as far as I thought they would, and they will go farther. Today the frontiers of journalism are no less open to young men and women fresh out of college, especially if they have the courage to poke down what appear to be narrow trails—regional magazines, city magazines, community magazines, airline magazines, trade magazines, specialty magazines and Sunday newspaper supplements. One trail leads to another; you make your own luck. Nobody's mother had heard of *The New Yorker, Time* or *Reader's Digest* when three young men—Harold Ross, Henry Luce and De Witt Wallace—first sent them out into the world in the 1920s.

ACKNOWLEDGMENTS

I warmly thank Anne Gilbert for her sensitivity and skill in transcribing most of the tapes that constituted the raw material of this book and retyping the chapters as they were revised.

P 5–6. "AIDS Tears Lives of the African Family," by John Tierney. *The New York Times*, Sept. 17, 1990.

P 6–8. "Joe Franklin, Maestro of Mess, Moves It." Ibid, May 23, 1991.

P 9–10. "Famous P.R. Man Fights 'So-Called Progress.'" Ibid, Nov. 6, 1991.

P 11. "Chessmanship: How to Kibitz Like a Master." Ibid, Oct. 15, 1990.

P 14–15. "Behind Monty Hall's Doors: Puzzle, Debate and Answer?" Ibid, July 31, 1991.

P 21–22. "Hers," by Jennifer Allen. *The New York Times*, May 13, 1982.

P 32. "Decisions, Decisions," by Kevin McKean. *Discover*, June 1985. Reprinted by permission.

P 35–37. Class blackboard drawings by Kevin McKean, recreated by his nine-year-old daughter, Kyle McKean, on her Macintosh computer using Kid Pix.

P 36–39, 40–41. "The Frontiers of Cancer Research," by Kevin McKean. Published by Memorial Sloan-Kettering Cancer Center, May 1989.

P 42–43. "E. O. Wilson: It's All in the Genes," by Kevin McKean. *Discover*, December 1982. Reprinted by permission.

P 44–45. "Special Report on Cardio–Vascular Research," by Kevin McKean. Bristol-Myers Squibb Co., March 1991.

P 58–59. Gardner Botsford. *The New Yorker*, Dec. 28, 1992 / January 4, 1993.

P 82–83. "Bush: As the Loss Sinks In," by Maureen Dowd. *The New York Times*, Nov. 7, 1992.

P 84–85. "Coolidge," by H. L. Mencken, from *The Vintage Mencken*, gathered by Alistair Cooke. Vintage Books (paper). Copyright © 1955 by Alfred A. Knopf, Inc. Reprinted by permission of the publisher.

P 92–94. "Goodman Ace: Words Fool Me," by Mark Singer. From *Mr. Personality*, Alfred A. Knopf, 1989. Originally in *The New Yorker*.

P 94–95. "Brennan Brothers: Supers," by Mark Singer. Ibid.

P 98–99. From "Funny Money," by Mark Singer. Alfred A. Knopf, 1985. Originally in *The New Yorker*.

P 101–102. "Predilections," by Mark Singer. From *The New Yorker*, Feb. 6, 1989.

P 106–107. *American Places*, by William Zinsser. HarperCollins 1992.

P 119. By Red Smith. From *The Red Smith Reader*, edited by Dave Anderson. Random House, 1982.

P 134. "Have We Become Fitness Crazed?" by Janice Kaplan. *Vogue*, March 1982.

P 135. "I Want to Go Home," by Janice Kaplan. *Self*, May 1990.

P 142–143. *Life on the Mississippi*, by Mark Twain.

P 143–144. *Out of Africa*, by Isak Dinesen. Random House, 1937.

P 144–145. *A River Runs Through It*, by Norman MacLean. University of Chicago Press, 1976.

P 148–151. "Losing Ground," by Sue Halpern. From *Audubon*, July–August 1992.

P 152. "Strip-Mine Shell Game," by Ted Williams. *Audubon*, November–December 1992.

P 156–157. "A Field Guide to Roger Tory Peterson," by William Zinsser. *Audubon*, November–December 1992.

P 165–166. "A Caring State," by Richard Ewald. *Vermont Magazine*, September–October 1992.

P 167. "Sending a Message," by Bill Porter. Ibid. March–April 1991.

P 168–169. "Colliding with the Moose," by Alan Pistorius. Ibid. September–October 1991.

P 169–170. "Mosquito Heaven," by Alan Pistorius. Ibid. May–June 1992.

P 172. "Townscape: St. Johnsbury," by Bernier L. Mayo. Ibid. November–December 1992.

P 174. "Poised on the Cusp of the Universe," by Jerry Gibbs. Ibid. January–February 1992.

P 176–177. The Yale graduate who co-founded *The Journal of Contemporary Art*, though not a student of mine, happened to be the one who most closely exemplified the notions of looking for and learning from a first job in journalism that I did recommend to my students. He is my son John Zinsser.

WILLIAM ZINSSER is a writer, editor and teacher. He was on the *New York Herald Tribune* from 1946 to 1959 and then became a free-lance writer and a columnist for *Life* and other magazines. During the 1970s he taught writing at Yale, where he was master of Branford College. From 1979 to 1987 he was general editor of the Book-of-the-Month Club. A lifelong traveler, he now writes frequently about such places as Yemen, Bali and Timbuktu. His 15 books, ranging in subject from jazz to baseball, include *On Writing Well*, now in its fifth edition, *Writing to Learn* and *American Places*. A fourth-generation New Yorker, he lives in his hometown with his wife, Caroline Zinsser.